**New Directions for
Community Colleges**

Arthur M. Cohen
EDITOR-IN-CHIEF

Caroline Q. Durdella
Nathan R. Durdella
ASSOCIATE EDITORS

Amy Fara Edwards
MANAGING EDITOR

D1524281

Applying College Change Theories to Student Affairs Practice

C. Casey Ozaki
Robin L. Spaid
EDITORS

Number 174 • Summer 2016
Jossey-Bass
San Francisco

APPLYING COLLEGE CHANGE THEORIES TO STUDENT AFFAIRS PRACTICE
C. Casey Ozaki, Robin L. Spaid (eds.)
New Directions for Community Colleges, no. 174

Arthur M. Cohen, Editor-in-Chief
Caroline Q. Durdella, Nathan R. Durdella, Associate Editors
Amy Fara Edwards, Managing Editor

NEW DIRECTIONS FOR COMMUNITY COLLEGES (ISSN 0194-3081, electronic ISSN 1536-0733) is part of The Jossey-Bass Higher and Adult Education Series and is published quarterly by Wiley Subscription Services, Inc., A Wiley Company, at Jossey-Bass, One Montgomery St., Ste. 1200, San Francisco, CA 94104. POSTMASTER: Send address changes to New Directions for Community Colleges, Jossey-Bass, One Montgomery St., Ste. 1200, San Francisco, CA 94104.

SUBSCRIPTIONS cost $89 for individuals in the U.S., Canada, and Mexico, and $113 in the rest of the world for print only; $89 in all regions for electronic only; $98 in the U.S., Canada, and Mexico for combined print and electronic; $122 for combined print and electronic in the rest of the world. Institutional print only subscriptions are $335 in the U.S., $375 in Canada and Mexico, and $409 in the rest of the world; electronic only subscriptions are $335 in all regions; combined print and electronic subscriptions are $402 in the U.S., $442 in Canada and Mexico, and $476 in the rest of the world.

Cover design: Wiley
Cover Images: © Lava 4 images | Shutterstock

EDITORIAL CORRESPONDENCE should be sent to the Editor-in-Chief, Arthur M. Cohen, at 1749 Mandeville Lane, Los Angeles, CA 90049. All manuscripts receive anonymous reviews by external referees.

New Directions for Community Colleges is indexed in CIJE: Current Index to Journals in Education (ERIC), Contents Pages in Education (T&F), Current Abstracts (EBSCO), Ed/Net (Simpson Communications), Education Index/Abstracts (H. W. Wilson), Educational Research Abstracts Online (T&F), ERIC Database (Education Resources Information Center), and Resources in Education (ERIC).

Microfilm copies of issues and articles are available in 16mm and 35mm, as well as microfiche in 105mm, through University Microfilms Inc., 300 North Zeeb Road, Ann Arbor, MI 48106-1346.

Contents

EDITORS' NOTES

As one of the most widely researched issues in higher education, student retention commands the attention of leaders across all sectors (Tinto, 2006–2007). The contentious issues of retention, graduation, and the completion agenda have surfaced in the debate about the costs and value of a college degree. Intrinsic to this debate are those practices and programs designed to support student success and graduation. The last issue of *New Directions for Community Colleges* that reviewed this topic was written in 2005. Editors Helfgot and Culp (2005) billed the issue as helping "to answer the questions about what really matters in community college student affairs" (Helfgot & Culp, 2005, p. 2). Prior to that, a seminal *New Directions* issue on student development edited by Deegan and O'Banion provided readers with "the history of student development practices, reviews of key issues that have emerged in the field, and proposes paths of action for the future" (Deegan & O'Banion, 1989, p. 1). These *New Directions* volumes have added to the knowledge base and laid the groundwork for a new volume that succinctly investigates theory and practice connected to the formative student development theories and the current college impact literature as they relate to community college students and the completion agenda.

The debate over student success, retention, and graduation is incomplete without a discussion about the body of theory and literature that is foundational to understanding the range of factors, contexts, and processes that influence college success and outcomes and undergird student services. Specifically, the literature related to student success and college impact presents conceptual models and theories that influence academic and student success programs in community colleges across the country (Astin, 1999, Tinto 1975, 1987, 1995; Kuh, 2005). For community colleges, this body of literature is a significant part of the research and theory that support the work of student services professionals and those who create policy for students. Despite the theoretical basis these models have provided, they were developed for and normed on students attending traditional, 4-year institutions. Therefore, the applicability of using these models and theories for understanding the experience of students at 2-year institutions may be problematic (Ashar & Skenes, 1993). Now community college leaders are poised to review current practices and services to ascertain whether the needs of current community college students are being met. A secondary,

NEW DIRECTIONS FOR COMMUNITY COLLEGES, no. 174, Summer 2016 © 2016 Wiley Periodicals, Inc.
Published online in Wiley Online Library (wileyonlinelibrary.com) • DOI: 10.1002/cc.20198

but no less important aspect for this issue is for researchers to determine if the current knowledge base is valid in moving the completion agenda forward.

Historically, the college impact literature was developed using a traditional-aged, homogeneous population of students at 4-year institutions. The theories of Astin (1999), Tinto (1975, 1987, 1995), and even Kuh (2005) do not address the issues that community college students face. Although these ideas have served as useful heuristics for understanding how students at 4-year institutions develop and the overall impact that college attendance has on persistence, questions have been raised about their applicability for the broad community college population and their suitability when applied to minority, nontraditional populations (Ashar & Skenes, 1993). In the decade following the Ashar and Skenes study, the terrain for community college student affairs has changed. Not only do community colleges serve different missions than the 4-year institutions do, they also serve different populations from those described by the current student success and college impact literature. The editors for this *New Directions* issue ask the questions: If theories and concepts are tools for student services personnel, but have not been developed with and for the student services personnel and populations at community colleges, how well do current models apply to and serve the professionals using these tools? If they are not applicable, what conceptual and theoretical tools do community college professionals have to assist them and the students they serve?

Applying College Change Theories to Student Affairs Practice offers a timely discussion of the foundational literature, concepts, and theories that undergird the student success practices, program development, and policy decisions enacted to guide and support students throughout their college experience. This issue examines the applicability of the body of literature currently available to student services personnel and leaders in community colleges. Chapters 1 and 2 review the seminal student development and college impact literature, examining how they have historically been developed and applied. Chapters 3 through 6 provide a block of chapters that explore the utility of this literature for specific community college student populations. In addition, alternative models and lenses are discussed. In Chapter 7 Gillett-Karam continues her commentary and critique of student development theory started in Chapter 1 and examines its implications for practice and practitioners. Finally, in Chapter 8, expanding on the Editors' Notes, the editors summarize each chapter and discuss commonalities and intersections across the issue providing implications for practice and recommendations for alternative perspectives that better align with the community college context and populations.

C. Casey Ozaki
Robin L. Spaid
Editors

NEW DIRECTIONS FOR COMMUNITY COLLEGES • DOI: 10.1002/cc

References

Ashar, H., & Skenes, R. (1993). Can Tinto's student departure model be applied to non-traditional students? *Adult Education Quarterly, 43*(2), 90–100.

Astin, A. (1999). Student involvement: A developmental theory for higher education. *Journal of College Student Development, 40*(5), 518–529.

Deegan, W. L., & O'Banion, T. (1989). Abstract. *New Directions for Community Colleges, 17*(3), 1.

Helfgot, S., & Culp, M. (2005). Editors' notes. *New Directions for Community Colleges, 131,* 1–5.

Kuh, G. (2005). *Student success in college: Creating conditions that matter.* San Francisco: Jossey-Bass.

Tinto, V. (1975). Dropout from higher education: A theoretical synthesis of recent research. *Review of Educational Research, 45,* 89–125.

Tinto, V. (1987). *Leaving college: Rethinking the causes and cures of student attrition.* Chicago: University of Chicago Press.

Tinto, V. (1995). *Leaving college: Rethinking the causes and cures of student attrition* (2nd ed.). Chicago: University of Chicago Press.

Tinto, V. (2006–2007). Research and practice of student retention. What's next? *College Student Retention, Research, Theory & Practice, 8*(1), 1–20.

C. CASEY OZAKI is an associate professor in Teaching and Learning at the University of North Dakota. She received her Ph.D in Higher Education from Michigan State University.

ROBIN L. SPAID is a professor at Morgan State University. She received her EdD in Junior College Administration from Virginia Polytechnic Institute and State University.

1

By using a reconstructionist and critical theory approach, a review of student development theories demonstrates the problematic nature of such ideas as they continue to be used to shape student affairs practice in community colleges.

Moving from Student Development to Student Success

Rosemary Gillett-Karam

Student affairs and student services in American community colleges are at a standstill. In the last two decades, the demographics and identity of community college students have changed dramatically. Conventional student development theory fails to support the needs of today's demographically diverse community college students and, as a result, practitioners at these institutions and the programs that prepare them are ill suited to support these students in this context. This essay raises questions about the student development theories that undergird student affairs and student services practice at community colleges in relation to student success.

The Slow Progress in Community College Research and Student Affairs Practice

Most educational research on student development stems from the 4-year college experience, whereas community college research appeared in the 1970s, well past the genesis of student development theory. Contemporary community college scholars (Eddy, 2010, Nevarez, Wood, & Penrose, 2013; O'Banion, 1972, 1989; Shaw, Valadez & Rhoads, 1999) suggest that the community college of the past is no longer the community college of the future. Of students attending community colleges, 85% are considered nontraditional and marginal students whose cultural capital (i.e., assets rooted in cultural norms and relationships that promote social and economic mobility) has not been consistent with the cultural norms and expectations used to academically assess students, resulting in consistently underachievement in higher education (Bourdieu, 1990). Therefore, the lack of student success for many community college students is a

NEW DIRECTIONS FOR COMMUNITY COLLEGES, no. 174, Summer 2016 © 2016 Wiley Periodicals, Inc.
Published online in Wiley Online Library (wileyonlinelibrary.com) • DOI: 10.1002/cc.20199

foregone conclusion. Defining student success has remained both vague and ambiguous. A lack of consensus around its meaning allows a continuing reign of power and privilege that prevents either theorists or practitioners from recognizing and changing the concept as it affects college students. For example, consider the numbers of students who are *stuck* in remedial and developmental courses in community colleges: Their "ways of knowing" usually do not conform to the dominant hegemony of what constitutes *knowing* in our colleges currently. How and what students know and learn are culturally bound; they are an artifact of cultural capital and influence student success in higher education. When *how* and *what* students know do not align with college expectations or norms for learning, the student may experience a lack of belonging and an academic performance that leads to struggling in the classroom at best and attrition at worst.

Often labeled the "people's colleges," community colleges of the 21st century are a reflection of the composite of American diversity and multiculturalism. However, higher education continues to teach and provide student support much as it was in the 1960s and 1970s and, although a goal is to focus attention and programs on student needs, the culture of evidence does not reflect the truth of that statement. If community colleges are cultural texts (Shaw, Valadez, & Rhoads, 1999), evidence of cultural practice and norms, then the practice of student development theories are fixed or imposed upon students and do not reflect the "identities" of modern community college students. The call from higher education and community college researchers, therefore, should reflect substantive reformation of the dominant theories of student development tied to student development and involvement, student engagement, student identity and culture, and student access and success.

Reflective Practice and a Reconstructionist and Critical Theory Lens

As a member of an ethnic minority I have lived a life of repression, oppression, and resistance—as a young woman, I reluctantly followed the norm set out by my 100% White male professors. Recalling an incident as an undergraduate, I was called to "visit" with a professor who stared at me for what seemed to be an interminable time. The professor finally said to me, "What are YOU doing here? YOU don't belong." At the time, I did not know this was an educational system that failed me; I had not reflected on my own cultural capital. And, despite my bowing down to the dominant culture and its "truths," I began to ruminate on the "other" (DeBeauvoir, 1949) and consequently found scholars who, like me, were beginning to reflect on and dismantle inequality and loss of voice.

The underlying theme of this chapter is to reflect on dominant ideas about students, ask questions about student development theories, and examine the use of deterministic language usually associated with student development theory. I expect my readers to understand that theory is not religion and should not be worshipped as the "one right way." My approach to this critical essay is as a social reconstructionist and critical theorist; I believe our obligation to students is to overcome privilege and class hegemony that produce oppression and voicelessness. Learning, as advanced by Freire (1970), is a process of inquiry in which the student's curiosity allows her to invent and reinvent the world. Knowledge is not banked from professor to student; it is discovered by the student as he experiences the world. A student learns by doing and enjoys a college curriculum focused on taking social action, which parallels her experiences. Reconstructionists and critical theorists believe education is the medium that returns to the vision of equality, justice, and democracy in our society. McLaren & Jaramillo (2007) believed these principles "provide for a qualitatively better way of life for all through the construction of society based on non-exploitative relations and social justice" (p. 195). Using this lens to critically examine student development theory and practice based in these concepts facilitates exposure of the gaps in its current use and failure to mediate the equity, justice, and democracy that education should help achieve.

Social justice is a second defining theme of this chapter as I seek to explore the social construction of society and its evolution, beginning with student development as implemented from the 1930s through the 1980s. Social and behavioral sciences undergird most theoretical views of student development, whereas postmodernist and critical theory challenge student development views and theories. Both are discussed here. This essay raises these probing questions:

- How does reflective practice reveal the story of student development?
- How has student development theory been cataloged and focused? Who are the critics of these theories?
- How does the history of student development theory and its reforms affect student success in community colleges?
- What are the major theories of student development?
- How do college impact models redirect student services and student affairs structures in community colleges?
- How can a new vision (*unlearning and relearning*) of meeting student needs and student services attempt to redress issues of inequality, injustice, and indoctrination in community colleges?

These questions promote a view writ large about community colleges and their focus on students. There are conflicting views of student development (and its theories) and student professionals who guide offices and programs of student affairs. In the following discussion, readers are asked to conceptualize, deconstruct, and reconceptionalize the issues that represent conflicting views of students and their development—their bases for consideration and their bases for continuing inquiry. More specifically, community college practitioners are invited to reconsider their special role in the American community college and its role in forwarding reconstructed meaning for students.

Historical Emphasis on Students

One of the seminal texts on student development theory has undergone a philosophical repositioning. Evans, Forney, Guido, Patton, and Renn (2010) have reflected on their earlier foci and offered this apology: "The student development theory we included in the first edition of the book is inadequate to understand and work effectively with students of the 21st century" (p. xvii). This apology needs explanation and discussion among researchers and practitioners and in the following discussion is clarified to some extent.

Modern accounts of student development theories and research begin with 17th century American higher education and the idea that college presidents and professors were personally involved in the lives of their students, who, for the most part, were children of White, landed elite, studying to become ministers, lawyers, and politicians. However, as college presidents and professors began to separate themselves from their daily, nonacademic relationships with students a rift in academic versus student interaction began to occur. Although this separation seemed endemic, the question of who students were and what they needed to succeed became a central question to student development and student affairs. The separation between academic and student affairs became institutionalized around the mid-19th century.

Guided by the concept of *in loco parentis*, deans of students filled in for faculty who had removed themselves from personal involvement with students; the advent of the research university cemented this separation between academic affairs and student affairs. Acting "in place of the parent" meant acting on behalf of students and focused on controlling (not developing) students and their character building, usually based on Christian beliefs. Deans and their staff took on the role of administering to the needs of students.

Student affairs as a distinctive bureaucratic agency in colleges and universities began to examine and train for the idea of "meeting student needs." By the early 20th century, NASPA – Student Affairs Administrators in Higher Education (formerly National Association of Student Personnel Administrators) was formed; and other national conferences and journals, such as the American College Student Personnel Association and the *Journal of College Student Development*, would emerge as colleges and universities and their rising student populations grew. Students and their roles were not forgotten; they lived on campuses and their behavior and development were of interest to a new group of practitioners, student affairs professionals. According to some researchers the focal point for modern interpretation of student affairs begins with the American Council of Education's 1937 and

NEW DIRECTIONS FOR COMMUNITY COLLEGES • DOI: 10.1002/cc

1949, which provided guidance and vision for offices of student services and student affairs in colleges and universities. The SPPV statements continue to be in use in the modern period, some three-quarters of a century since their origin.

I offer here a critique of formal, professional training and the idea that student affairs practices may be unrelated to student development theories, particularly within 2-year institutions. This idea raises a second gap in the research about student growth and direction in college—how much do we really know about theory and practice and to what extent is theory used and explained as intended by practitioners? Bensimon (2007) discussed the lack of theory-to-practice connection as a tension that resulted in "the invisibility of practitioners in the discourse on student success" (p. 443). She posited that practitioners operationalize an implicit theory or translation of theory when working with students, usually unguided by formal theory and unrecognized by social theorists.

Many researchers, especially in the modern period (Bensimon, 2004; Cuyjet, 2006; Harper & Quaye, 2008; Tanaka, 2002), are cautious about the term "theory" attached to student development in higher education. The question of the meaning of theory becomes connected with the ideas of positivism and fixed paradigms as we consider the implicit and insinuating discourse of language and who is and who is not allowed to control language and thus represent "the learner." Although this critique is pertinent to all of higher education, its consequences for community colleges is especially relevant for this discussion. As we account for these theories, modern critiques will be added; these critiques are rooted in social reconstructionalism and critical pedagogy.

Modern Ideas Influencing Student Development Theory

Research-driven universities and their growth led to an introduction of the social sciences, namely psychology and sociology (e.g., Jung, 1971; Rogers, 1957; Skinner, 1953), which proposed a new paradigm for understanding human behavior—the notion that students learn both in and out of class. These researchers posed the question of *nature versus nurture* in their attempts to determine the effect of genetic and social environments on learning and behavior. This line of inquiry was extended to the exploration of how the collegiate environment influences the student across many outcomes, including their development. Although there is no proof of an original theorist who claims the discovery of student development theory, most would agree that Erikson (1950), Sanford (1967), and Feldman, Theodore, and Newcomb (1969) were early contributors to the field. Evident in the evolution of student development theory and research and its critique, researchers are aware of the social and economic construction of reality and the spectrum of understanding of how power and privilege can define who may be allowed or chosen to learn and for what reasons. The following review of student development and additional literatures confronts the applicability of these theories to practice at community colleges, specifically using the lens of social justice and remains acutely aware of the influence of power and privilege.

Psychosocial Stages of Development.   These theories have their origins in the concept of development and the idea of maturity and chronological age; students are thought to learn as they progress through various life stages. The following researchers and theories are foundational to this category of student development theory:

- Piaget (1948)—how children learn
- Erikson (1950)—eight age-based stages based on chronological age, infancy to later adulthood
- Chickering and Reisser (1993)—seven vectors of identity from developing competence to developing integrity
- Knefelkamp (1978)—practice-to-theory, challenge, support, and intervention
- Schlossberg (1989)—marginality and mattering/transition model of student development.

Critiques of these models focus on the question of hegemony and, for the most part, the absence of representation in early developmental models of a full array of diverse learners. Researchers today ask if the intentions of "creating healthy, socialized adults capable of succeeding in the workplace, and engaging with meaningful questions" (Chickering & Reisser, 1993) hide a well-meaning but hidden agenda that reproduces selected and hegemonic values based on cultural reproduction and logical conformism, ignoring social justice and democratic values. Bourdieu (1990) links these ideas with symbolic power, or the ability of the privileged to establish reality while ignoring multiple peoples or their unique cultures. Lucchesi (2013) explains, "While Chickering's theory has served as a 'universal truth' for 50 years, it is time for practitioners to think critically about the culture they reinforce (insinuate) when facilitating … identity development" (p. 8). Other writers who elaborate on the role of hegemony and its privileged values are Jones and Abes (2013), Tanaka (2002), and Torres, Jones, and Renn (2009). Shaw, Valadez, and Rhoads (1999) asks the question of the marginalization of students in community colleges and suggests recognition of the multiplicity of student identities.

Cognitive Structural.   Theories in this realm are interested in how students perceive and rationalize their experiences, including making meaning, and demonstrating morality.

- Fowler (1981)—faith development
- Gilligan (1982)—women's moral development
- Kegan (1982, 1994)—evolving understanding of self
- Baxter Magolda (1999)—epistemological reflections

NEW DIRECTIONS FOR COMMUNITY COLLEGES • DOI: 10.1002/cc

Critics of these theories suggest a discussion of the way students think, but not *what or how* they think. Criticism, for example, may focus on Piaget (1948), whose ideas of cognitive structural development were based on male children whom he was said to "underestimate;" he never translated his theory to the practice of teaching or learning. What he did, however, was to reintroduce cognitive theorists, including Vygotsky (1962) to social constructivism. Vygotsky's theory of social development involved teachers who provided support or assistance to students (scaffolding) until the student learner could work independently. The introduction of social constructivism to cognitivism emphasized the aspect of learning that involved student and teacher learning from one another.

Later critics of cognitive-structural theories, such as Kodama (2002), argued that if the context remains entangled with a privileged society, the student is forced to learn how to survive in an oppressive society. Shaw, Valadez, and Rhoads (1999) would conclude that in community colleges the presence of the *habitus* (the guarantee of indoctrinating past ideas of correctness) can be juxtaposed with *resistance* (responses to constraint and domination) stemming from classicism. These authors suggest, however, that resistance is difficult for students to act upon. For example, low-income students can resist professorial dicta but find themselves unable to prevail, leading to stopouts and dropouts in colleges. A significant proportion of community college students come from more powerless communities and could have experiences such as those described.

Person–Environment.   The person–environment research is interested in relations between students and their environments, behavior becomes a social function, such as career planning, between the student and the environment.

- Banning (1978)—campus ecology
- Astin (1984)—student involvement; introduced person–environment models to student development theories
- Holland (1985, 1992)—vocational personalities

Critics focus on issues such as campus and institutional environments that pigeonhole students based on testing. Career planning and vocations were, and continue to be, decided on the basis of class, race, and socioeconomic status. No doubt my own "discovery" of place reflected this idea: Women of my generation were not lawyers, doctors, engineers, or astronauts. They were nurses, hairdressers, and secretaries. Minorities did not have the same characteristics as Whites, and entrance exams at colleges and universities demonstrated "they" would not fit the example of the American college student. At another level of "typecasting," Dougherty (1994) elaborates on a predisposition to disparage community colleges' emphases on vocational (rather than transfer) education; later he would reconsider this idea (2006), taking note of the importance of modern workforce needs and multiple community college missions. As institutions that are dedicated to the preparation of student to enter into trade vocations and in many states is the sole institution type to provide developmental coursework, research has demonstrated the cooling out phenomenon that reflects formal and informal practices that prevent students from progressing toward and achieving their educational goals (Clark, 1960).

Identity. Identity models are less oppressive than other models, mainly because the literature and research today continues to emphasize student identity as a basis for human agency. Torres, Jones, and Renn (2009) explains that identity is not only a personal reflection of self but also a reflection of self to others. She warned that student development theory moves slowly in its consideration and acknowledgment of the issues of power as the basis of self-worth. Previous theories simply adapted "true and tried" theories to new groups, whereas later ideas about underrepresented groups and their identities would question those reused theories, by expressing concepts such as integration, nuance, and holism (Abes, Jones, & McEwen, 2007; Baxter Magolda, 2004; Winkler-Wagner, 2013). These writers introduce and use the term *intersectionality* and identity. Identity is not "parsed" out or based on one single characteristic; rather, students claim experience in multiple and dynamic aspects of identity by exploring race, gender, class, sexual orientation, and religious preference simultaneously. These theorists include:

- Cross (1991)—Nigrescence
- Helms (1993)—White Identity Model
- Josselson (1973)—identity development in women
- Phinney (1990)—ethnic identity formation
- D'Augelli (1994)—lesbian/gay/bisexual identity development

We do not have multiple discussions on issues of identity concerning low income, first-generation, single-parent-working, veteran, and prisoner students. Identity models by community college researchers have been few (Strayhorn, 2012; Shaw, Valadez & Rhoads, 1999; Nevarez & Wood, 2010) and, for the most part, their models do not use intersectionality as the basis for community college student identity.

Typologies. Typological theories are concerned with individual differences and their characteristics, preferring to label individuals according to their types—who are students and how can we understand them? A few of the typology researchers include:

- Myers and Myers (1980)—personality types
- Holland (1985)—vocational personalities and environments
- Kolb (1984)—learning styles

Student affairs professionals can offer testing types based on personalities and learning types, but some researchers question the studied results of these practices? Does what is learned from Kolb and Myers and Myers student preferences or a hierarchy of certain personalities over others discourage agency from emerging? In leadership theory, for example, we take note that extroverts are more represented than introverts and that hiring groups may use this idea to choose one candidate over another.

Community college researchers, such as Cohen and Brawer (2008), Cohen, Brawer, and Kisker (2014), Roueche (1989), and Vaughan and Weisman (2006) discuss community college leaders from such perspectives. Bensimon and Neumann (1994), Eddy (2010), and Nevarez, Wood, and Penrose (2013) instead propose a multidimensional view for leaders of community colleges and raise questions about the continuing and overwhelming preponderance of White, male college presidents in community colleges and the underrepresentation of ethnic minorities and women in these roles. College impact models can provide insight into changing ideas for student affairs and student services in community colleges.

Using a reconstructionist and critical theory approach, the review of student development theories demonstrated the problematic nature of the foundational theoretical literature used to shape practice in student affairs at community colleges. Adopting complementary, accompanying, and, sometimes, simply different approaches and theories may divert from common practice or typical curricular approaches in preparation programs but are arguably necessary to providing an equitable education to community college students.

Reconceptualizing a New Approach

Adult learning theory and critical theory research and literature are promising alternatives for providing theoretical foundations for the development of community college student affairs practice and policy. The students these institutions serve are largely older-than-average, are juggling multiples roles, and often come to higher education from backgrounds that are incompatible with the norms in higher education. Therefore, these lenses are better positioned to help practitioners develop programs and policy that more effectively meet student needs. Perhaps researchers and professionals in community colleges and beyond need to engage in a process of unlearning the status quo and relearning new perspectives and approaches.

Learning Theory.   The consideration of learning theory introduces an accompanying view of student development—a significant one. Learning has been defined in complex and sometimes confounding language based on who is doing the defining. Passing on knowledge for life, in itself, is both a natural and familial phenomenon, but also involves a process that moves generations to contribute to themselves and society. How students learn is an age-old question that has been tackled by philosophers and by educational generalists. Brookfield and Holst (2010), Kincheloe, Slattery, and Steinberg (2000), Kincheloe (2008), and Merriam (2008) are contemporary researchers who pose this question. In general, learning theory derives from asking questions about how students learn and how they make use of learning. Teaching and learning frames an expectation about student learning taken up by critical theory and critical pedagogy constructs.

Critical Theory.   Critical theory is the idea that theories can be criticized by those who raise questions about history, philosophy, and man. Postmodernism proposes that the "world is essentially fragmented, and that what passes for theoretical generalizations are really only context specific insights produced by particular discourse communities" Peca (2000). Critical theory is characterized by challenging one-sided, idealist, and reductionist positions. It challenges what is frequently "taken for granted socially and culturally; asking questions of things that are otherwise considered to be self-evident" (p. 1).

Kincheloe, Slattery, & Steinberg (2000) argue that the political and ethical dimensions must involve critical thinking, or the "ability of individuals to disengage themselves from the tacit assumptions of discursive practices and power relations in order to exert more conscious control over their everyday lives" (p. 24). Giroux (2006) adds:

> (e)ducation should be about the following: scholars who not only defend higher education as a democratic public sphere, but who also see themselves as both scholars and citizen activists willing to connect their research, teaching, and service to broader democratic concerns over equality, justice, and an alternative vision of what the university and society might become. (p. 278)

What theories and practices about students and their academic development might become—not just the way the world is, but what it might become—focuses this chapter.

A new vision, involving *unlearning and relearning*, of meeting student needs and student services attempts to redress issues of inequality, injustice and indoctrination in community colleges. Toffler (1981) wrote,

> The illiterate of the 21st century will not be those who cannot read and write, but those who cannot learn, *unlearn, and relearn*. You see, it's much less about the corporate history, the corporate culture, or even the environment in which we introduce the concepts of human capital optimization and organizational development coaching—it's about each individual opening their mind to the possibility of learning something new." Our interest in students stems from this idea—openness to learning something new from our college students, and relearning the processes to bring change to meet a changing student identity. (p. 367)

Modern researchers are focused on "what we might become" when we face injustice at all levels of education. In the concluding chapter efforts are made to suggest a new focus on students and their changing identities and needs in the American community college.

References

Abes, E., Jones, S., & McEwen. M. (2007). Reconceptualizing the model of multiple dimensions of identity. *Journal of College Student Development, 45*, 612–632.

Astin, A. W. (1984). Student involvement: A developmental theory for higher education. *Journal of College Student Personnel, 25*, 297–308.

Banning, J. H. (Ed). (1978). *Campus ecology: A perspective for student affairs.* Cincinnati: National Association of Student Personnel Administrators.

Baxter Magolda, M. (2004). Evolution of a constructivist conceptualization of epistemological reflection. *Educational Psychologist, 39*, 31–42.

Baxter Magolda, M. B. (1999). *Creating contexts for learning and self-authorship: Constructive developmental pedagogy.* Nashville: Vanderbilt University Press.

Bensimon, E. M. (2004). Closing the achievement gap in higher education: An organizational learning perspective. In A. Kezar (Ed.), *Organizational learning in higher education, 131.* San Francisco: Jossey-Bass.

Bensimon, E. M. (2007). The underestimated significance of practitioner knowledge in the scholarship of student success. *The Review of Higher Education, 30*(4), 441–469.

Bensimon, E., & Neumann, A. (1994). *Redesigning collegiate leadership.* Baltimore, MD: Johns Hopkins University Press.

Bourdieu, P. (1990). *Language and symbolic power.* Cambridge, UK: Polity Press.

Brookfield, S. & Holst, J. (2010). *Radicalizing learning: adult education for a just world.* San Francisco: Jossey-Bass.

Chickering, A. W., & Reisser, L. (1993). *Education and identity* (2nd ed.). San Francisco: Jossey-Bass.

Clark, B. (1960). *The open door college.* NY: McGraw Hill.

Cohen, A. M., & Brawer, F. B. (2008, 2014). *The American community college* (5th ed.). San Francisco: Jossey-Bass.

Cohen, A. M., Brawer, F. B., & Kisker, C. B. (2014). *The American community college* (6th ed.). San Francisco: Jossey-Bass

Cross, W. E., Jr. (1991). *Shades of black: Diversity in African American identity.* Philadelphia: Temple University Press.

Cuyjet, M. J. (2006). African American college men. In M. J. Cuyjet & Associates (Eds.), *African American men in college* (pp. 3–23). San Francisco: Jossey-Bass.

D'Augelli, A. R. (1994). "Identity Development and Sexual Orientation: Toward a Model of Lesbian, Gay, and Bisexual Development." In E. J. Trickett, R. J. Watts, & D. Birman (Eds.), *Human Diversity: Perspectives on People in Context.* San Francisco: Jossey-Bass.

DeBeauvoir, S. (1949). *The Second Sex* (H. M. Parshley, Trans., 1972). Penguin. *Development theory into the academic classroom.*

Dougherty, K. J. (1994). *The contradictory college.* Albany: State University of New York Press.

Eddy, P. L. (2010). *Community college leadership: A multidimensional model for leading change.* Sterling, VA: Stylus.

Erikson, E. (1950). *Childhood and society.* New York. Norton.

Evans, N. J., Forney, D. S., Guido, F., Patton, L. D., & Renn, K. A. (2010). *Student development in college: Theory, research, and practice* (2nd ed.). San Francisco: Jossey-Bass.

Feldman, K., Theodore, M., & Newcomb, T. M. (1969). *The impact of college on students.* San Francisco: Jossey and Bass.

Fowler, J. W. (1981). *Stages of faith: The psychology of human development and the quest for meaning.* New York: Harper Collins.

Freire, P. (1970). *Pedagogy of the oppressed.* NY: Continuum.

Gilligan, C. (1982). *In a different voice: Psychological theory and women's development.* Cambridge: Harvard University Press.

Giroux, H. (2006). *America on the Edge: Henry Giroux on Politics, Education, and Culture.* London: Palgrave Macmillan.

Harper, S., & Quaye, S. (2008). *Student engagement in higher education: Theoretical perspectives and practical approaches for diverse populations.* New York: Routledge.

Helms, J. E. (1993). *Black and white racial identity: Theory, research and practice.* Westport, CT: Praeger.

Holland, J. L. (1985, 1992). *Making vocational choices: A theory of vocational personalities and work environments* (2nd ed.). Odessa, FL: Psychological Assessment Resources.

Jones, S., & Abes, E. (2013). *Identity development of college students: Advancing frameworks for multiple dimensions of identity.* San Francisco: Jossey-Bass.

Josselson, R. E. (1973). Psychodynamic aspects of identity formation in college women. *Journal of Youth and Adolescence, 2*(1), 3–52.

Jung, C. (1971). Psychological types. In R. E. C. Hull & H. G. Baynes (Eds.), *The collected works of C.G. Jung. 6.* Princeton: Princeton University Press.

Kegan, R. (1982). *The evolving self.* Cambridge: Harvard University Press.

Kegan, R. (1994). *In over our heads: The mental demands of modern life.* Cambridge: Harvard University Press.

Kincheloe, J. (2008). Critical pedagogy primer (2nd ed.). New York: Peter Lang.

Kincheloe, J. L., Slattery, P., & Steinberg, S. R. (2000). *Contextualizing teaching: Introduction to the foundations of education.* New York: Longman.

Knefelkamp, L. L. (1978). *A reader's guide to student development theory: A framework for understanding, a framework for design.* Unpublished manuscript.

Kodama, C. (2002). Working with Asian American college students. *New Directions for Student Services, 97,* 45–9.

Kolb, D. A. (1984). *Experiential learning: Experience as the source of learning and development.* Upper Saddle River, NJ: Prentice Hall.

Lucchesi, M. L. (2013). *Hegemony within student affairs: The interpretive nature of college student development theory.* Master's thesis, DePaul University. Retrieved from http://via.library.depaul.edu/soe_etd/47

Lucchesi, M. L. (2013). *Hegemony within student affairs: The interpretive nature of college student development theory.* College of Education. Paper 47. http://via.library.depaul.edu/soe_etd/47

McLaren, P., & Jaramillo, N. (2007). *Pedagogy and praxis.* Rotterdam: Sense Publishers.

Merriam, S. (2008). *Qualitative research.* SF: Jossey-Bass.

Myers, I. B., & Myers, P. B. (1980). *Gift differing: Understanding personality type.* Palo Alto: Consulting Psychological Press.

Nevarez, C., & Wood, J. L. (2010). *Community college leadership and administration: Theory, practice and change.* New York, NY: Peter Lang.

Nevarez, C., Wood, L., & Penrose, R. (2013). *Leadership theory and the community college.* Sterling, VA: Stylus.

O'Banion, T. (1972). An academic advising model. *American Association of Junior Colleges Journal, 42,* 62–64.

O'Banion, T. (1989). *Innovation in the community college.* New York: American Council on Education.

Peca, K. (2000). *Critical theories in education.* http://files.eric.ed.gov/fulltext/ED455564.pdf

Phinney, J. (1990). Ethnic identity in adolescents and adults. *Psychology Bulletin, 108*(3), 499–514.

Piaget, J. (1948). *The psychology of Intelligence*. London: Routledge.

Rogers, C.R. (1957). The necessary and sufficient conditions of therapeutic personality change. *Journal of Consulting and Clinical Psychology*, 21: 95–103.

Roueche, J. (1989). *Shared vision*. Washington, DC: AACC.

Sanford, N. (1967). *The student in the total learning environment*. New York: Wiley.

Schlossberg, N. K. (1989). Marginality and mattering: Key issues in building community. In D. C. Roberts (Ed.), *Designing campus activities to foster a sense of community* (pp. 5–15). New Directions for Student Services, 48. San Francisco: Jossey-Bass.

Shaw, K., Valadez, J., & Rhoads, R. (Eds.). (1999). *Community colleges as cultural texts*. Albany: State University of New York Press.

Skinner, B. F. (1953). *Science and human behavior*. New York: Macmillan.

Strayhorn, T. L. (2012). Satisfaction and retention among African American men at two-year community colleges. *Community College Journal of Research and Practice*, 36(5), 358–375.

Student Personnel Point of View, SPPV(1937, 1949). American Council on Education.

Tanaka, G. (2002). Higher education's self-reflexive turn: Toward an intercultural theory of student development. *Journal of Higher Education*, 73, 263–266.

Toffler, A. (1981). Education and the future: An interview. *Social Education*, 45(6), 422–426.

Torres, V., Jones, S., & Renn, K. (2009). Identity development theories in student affairs: Origins, current status, and new approaches. *Journal of College Student Development*, 50(6), 577–596. doi:10.1353/csd.0.0102

Vaughan, G. & Weisman, I. (2006). *The community college presidency*. Washington, DC: American Association of Community Colleges.

Vygotsky, L. S. (1962). *Thought and language*. Cambridge: MIT Press.

Winkler-Wagner, R. (2013). *Get real. The process of validating research across racial lines*. New York, NY: Palgrave.

ROSEMARY GILLETT-KARAM *is Director of the Community College Leadership Program at Morgan State University. She received her Ph.D. from University of Texas at Austin.*

2

This chapter critically examines the fit and applicability of foundational college impact theories to the community college context and students. Implications for the literature and campuses are explored.

College Impact Theories Past and Present

C. Casey Ozaki

For the past 40 years, *New Directions for Community Colleges* (NDCC) has concerned itself with the issues, trends, and concerns of community colleges. As a result, it is one of the few publications and sources of community college literature that has attended to the student services and student affairs sector. In 1989, Deegan and O'Banion's NDCC volume, *Perspectives on Student Development,* examined the underpinnings of student affairs emphasizing the importance of counseling and a humanistic approach to student services. They also recognized the impact that *The Student Personnel Point of View* (American Council on Education, 1937, 1949) had on the development of the field. Finally, their synonymous use of the label *student development professionals* for *student affairs professionals* and *student services personnel* demonstrates the importance of student development literature and theory as foundations to the field as well.

In 2005, Helfgot and Culp updated NDCC readers and community college professionals with their volume, *Community College Student Affairs: What Really Matters?* This volume focused on student success and the alignment of the role of student affairs and support services with the core mission of 2-year institutions—student learning. In conjunction with a student success focus, assessment of programmatic efficacy and student learning and outcomes were touted as unavoidable areas of change and attention for the future. With little else in the literature that specifically examined the intersection between student affairs and community colleges, it is curious that a critical examination of the theoretical literature and models that underscore this work is not addressed more readily.

Currently, estimates indicate that over 50% of higher education students attend a community college, but only 46% of those with the goal of a degree or certificate achieve that goal or transfer to a baccalaureate

NEW DIRECTIONS FOR COMMUNITY COLLEGES, no. 174, Summer 2016 © 2016 Wiley Periodicals, Inc.
Published online in Wiley Online Library (wileyonlinelibrary.com) • DOI: 10.1002/cc.20200

institution within 6 years (American Association of Community Colleges, 2012, 2014). These problematic completion rates elicited a call from President Obama (2009) for increased graduation and transfer by 2020 and a response from the American Association of Community College's 21st-Century Commission on the Future of Community College's (2012) whose first recommendation is to increase completion rates by 50% by 2020. This policy push places 2-year institutions under significant pressure to produce aligned outcomes and improvement in completion and success rates. Therefore, it is the responsibility of all personnel who work with students to help them achieve their academic goals and make progress on the completion agenda. In fact, it may be that student services personnel are most likely to be tasked with student success policy and initiatives. If the primary theoretical basis for retention and success was not generated from the community college context, then are these models an appropriate conceptual foundation for those who work with students?

The significance of the student development literature to student affairs practice and of college impact literature to student success has been foundational to the field, but these bodies of literature were developed with 4-year college students and settings as the data source. Yet, community colleges and their student population differ in many ways from traditional 4-year institutions. Therefore, it is critical to question and explore the applicability of these "theories and models of student change" (Pascarella & Terenzini, 2005, p. 17) to this population and institution type. In Chapters 1 and 7 of this volume, Gillett-Karam explores similar questions specifically focused on student development theory. To complement her investigation, in this chapter, I begin the necessary process of examining the fit and application of the college impact literature in a community college context.

College Impact Literature

The body of literature identified as college impact theory focuses on *How College Affects Students* (Pascarella & Terenzini, 2005). Well into its fourth decade, the literature attempts to evaluate and identify the impact that the college experience and environment have on student outcomes. In other words, how does college change and affect students in the short and long term? As an expansive body of research on the topic has been amassed and developed over time, researchers have developed models and theories to describe critical factors and interactions that influence student change.

College impact theory is one of two distinct areas of study. Both focus on the influence of the college environment and experience on student change and outcomes but reflect different categories of outcomes that a student might experience. First, the student development literature examines the ways that college influences psychological, affective, and cognitive development; in other words, student maturity. Theorists and researchers

NEW DIRECTIONS FOR COMMUNITY COLLEGES • DOI: 10.1002/cc

have presented scores of models and theories that describe and investigate the ways that students' identity, morals and values, cognition, and epistemological change over time and are influenced by college environment and experiences.

Second, the college impact literature focuses on the behavioral outcomes that result from college attendance. Educational and occupational attainment, income, career choice, leadership, attitudes, and values all fall within this category. Pascarella and Terenzini (2005) describe this family of models as focusing

> on the environmental and *inter*individual origin of student change, which need not be seen as developmental. These *college impact* models emphasize change associated with the characteristics of the institutions students attend (between-college effects) or with the experiences students have while enrolled (within-college effects). These models tend to be eclectic and to identify and evaluate several sets of variables presumed to influence one or more aspects of change. These sets may be student-related (such as gender, academic achievement, socioeconomic status, race-ethnicity), structural and organizational (such as institutional size, type of control, selectivity, curricular mission), or environmental (for example, the academic, cultural, social, or political climate created by faculty and students on a campus). (p. 18)

College impact models focus on the *source* of student change. Ideally, these models are functional and flexible to help describe and explain student change across institutional type and student populations, but, as I discuss, this has not always been the case.

Over the nearly 4 decades of research in these areas, the literature has changed and developed. Initially, most studies were conducted using samples of white, male college students at 4-year institutions. Since the origin of this body of literature, the population of students and variation of college contexts being studied have expanded. Now the literature reflects the diversity of college student race, ethnicity, age, income, work and attendance status, religion, gender, sexual orientation, and commuter status, to name a few. The research has also broadened to examine the influence of cocurricular and classroom experiences, different institutional types, and varying backgrounds and preparation for college on student outcomes.

Recent research has demonstrated that the presence of formal curriculum on community colleges in student affairs and higher education master's programs, is largely absent (Latz & Royer, 2014). If community colleges are viewed as major players for the completion agenda but remain less visible across graduate preparation curricula, the the preparation of professionals for and at this institutional type is challenging and potentially problematic. Furthermore, as graduate education in the fields of higher education and student affairs have developed and formalized foundational literature, college impact has been included and canonized as instrumental.

Yet, despite the growth and expansion of the literature, only recently have theorists attempted to explore in depth how students at 2-year institutions fit into the models and theories.

Models and Theories. The following models and theories have served as building blocks of the college impact literature. Beginning in the 1970s researchers began to explore and focus on the intersection between students' experiences, persistence, and the environment—particularly the college environment. Beginning with Astin's Theory of Involvement (1985) through more recent approaches, I discuss the major tenets of these models and examine their use and applicability to the 2-year institution and student population.

I-E-O Model and the Theory of Involvement. Astin's (1970a, 1970b, 1975, 1991; Pascarella & Terenzini, 2005) Input-Environment-Outcomes (I-E-O) model has been one of most enduring and influential models that assists researchers and practitioners in examining the factors influencing student outcomes. Rather than a theoretical model focus on explaining change, I-E-O has served more as a conceptual or methodological guide or framework (Pascarella & Terenzini, 2005). The three elements of the model represent the category of factors that may influence the effects of college on students. *Inputs* are the demographic, personal, family, peer, social, and academic characteristics and experiences that students bring to college. This category allows researchers to assess how much of student outcomes are accounted for by variables they bring to college and, also, how those variables intersect with the college environment. The *Environment* element represents the people, programs, policies, cultures, and structures that students encounter at college; these reflect the range of experiences and factors that may affect student outcomes. Finally, the *Outcomes* dimension is an umbrella category for factors such as characteristics, knowledge, behavior, attitudes, values, etc. In addition to providing a structure of examining the impact of the college environment on student change and growth, the value of this model is the potential to provide data and findings to faculty, staff, and administrators that make decisions about resources, programs, and policy on campus.

Underscoring the I-E-O model is the complementary assertion that *students learn by becoming involved* (Astin, 1985). Five basic postulates help to explain this theory: (a) involvement requires psychological and physical investment and energy; (b) involvement is varied and individual—different students, differing levels of involvement, and different objects of involvement; (c) involvement is both quantitative and qualitative; (d) how much learning and development occurs is proportional to the quantity and quality of involvement; and (e) the effectiveness of policy and practice is predicated on its ability to promote involvement (Astin, 1985).

One of the reasons Astin's model and theory have endured and continue to be relevant to the study and practice of college impact is their flexibility. Inputs, environment, and outcomes are elements consistent across

institutional type and student population. The I-E-O elements are suffi-
ciently general enough to be applied across contexts, but the emphasis of
involvement for student change/development may be overstated for nonres-
idential community colleges. These students are known to be less active and
involved, psychologically and physically, on campus, and for their external
lives (e.g., job, family, children, etc.) to have a greater impact relative to the
campus environment. This differs from the assumption of involvement at
residential, 4-year colleges.

Theory of Student Departure.   Tinto's (1987, 1993, 2012) model of institutional impact includes the intersection between the institution and student, but the focus is narrowed to the outcome of student withdrawal. The
model illustrates the theoretical longitudinal trajectory a student makes
through an institution. First, as students enter a college Tinto suggested
that they bring a series of preentry characteristics (i.e., family, prior schooling, skills and abilities) that shape their intentions and goal commitments.
Second, students engage (or not) in the academic and social systems within
the institution. According to Tinto, these formal and informal encounters
are critical, leading to or away from the academic and social integration and
socialization that is the cornerstone for the veracity of institutional and goal
commitments that precede student departure.

After its initial publication, the application of the model to nontraditional populations and institutional types other than 4-year residential colleges was heavily criticized (Bean & Metzner, 1985; Tierney, 2000). These
criticisms of Tinto's model suggest that it does not accurately take into account the influences of external commitments in detail (Cabrera, Nora,
Castaneda, & Hengstler, 1992) and, therefore, is not as applicable to nontraditional student populations (Napoli & Wortman, 1996, 1998). Moreover,
there continue to be questions about Tinto's model providing a full explain
of retention in relation to minority student departure (Rendon, Jalomo, &
Nora, 2000; Tierney, 2000). Underrepresented and minority students are
known to be heavily involved in their external commitments. Therefore,
given the high proportion of these students enrolled at community colleges (Tinto, 1993), the appropriateness of Tinto's model for this sector is
questionable. Similarly, researchers have also suggested that the concepts
of academic and social integration may rely on false assumptions about
what community college students' academic and social integration looks
like (Tierney, 2000), suggesting that Tinto's concepts were based on the traditional, residential 4-year institution and is, therefore, inappropriate for
the 2-year institution student population. For students at residential institutions, there is an emphasis on social integration through on-campus
activities and experiences such as residential living, student organizations,
student employment, and peer interactions (Tinto, 1993). Yet, as previously
discussed, students at 2-year institutions have more external obligations
(e.g., family, children, job, etc.) and are more likely to locate their social
lives outside of the institution and off campus. Studies on integration and

involvement for 2-year and commuter college students demonstrate a different pattern given the importance of students' external lives. As opposed to students from residential campuses, involvement integration is focused on academic involvement (e.g., interaction with faculty, time spent in the library, in-class attendance, and interaction with peers).

In the most recent edition of Tinto's (2012) *Leaving College*, he revised his discussion of the model's elements to emphasize the application of the model to commuter and community colleges. In this discussion, although he still talks about external commitments having detrimental effects on student intention and withdraw, Tinto does acknowledge and discuss in more depth that for some students (e.g., adult, married, etc.) external commitments can be critical motivators and elements. In fact, he devotes more space and discussion to differences by individual student and institutional type than previously. He summarizes the patterns of departure:

> Compared to patterns of departure in largely residential institutions, departure from community colleges appears to be influenced less by social events than by strictly academic matters ... and more influenced by external forces which shape the character of students' lives off campus than by events internal to the campus ... Two-year college students, like commuting students generally, are much more likely to be working while in college, attending part-time rather than full-time, and/or living at home while in college than are students in the four-year sector. They, too, are likely to experience a wide range of competing external pressures on their time and energies and to be unable to spend significant amounts of time on campus interacting with other students and members of the staff. (Tinto, 2012, p. 78)

Recommendations for institutional action reflect the ways that 2-year colleges may affect students. Four recommendations are made: (a) given the importance of classroom involvement for this population, constructing classroom communities is critical; (b) although students spend less time on campus, the on-campus environment should not be neglected and should provide as much opportunity for involvement as possible; (c) bridging the gap between college and external communities is especially important because external commitments and relationships are preeminent for these students; and (d) the varied participation patterns that exist for 2-year college students require these institutions to provide flexible and extended services (Tinto, 2012).

Tinto's (1985) Theory of Departure has been instrumental in helping researchers and practitioners understand the role the institution has in the withdrawal process or retention of students. It remains a fundamental and formative heuristic for the exploration of college impact on student success. Yet, it has been heavily criticized for narrowly reflecting one sector of higher education, 4-year residential institutions. Although Tinto's thinking about the applicability of the model has evolved over time (Tinto, 2012), what is less clear is whether the model is used and taught from this expanded perspective.

Nontraditional Student Attrition.   Bean and Metzner (1985, 1987) took issue with previous models that attempted to assess the impact of college on student attrition and retention. They argued that these models put too much emphasis on social variables that are less relevant to "nontraditional" students and their college experiences. In response, they proposed (1985) and tested (1987) an alternative conceptual framework for nontraditional students that included academic, background, psychological, and environmental variables. They theorized that the environmental variables would have the most effect on nontraditional student withdrawal decisions. Bean and Metzner's 1987 research on the model with nontraditional (commuter, part-time) students found that dropout was a function of academic reasons and commitment to the institution and that social variables played a much smaller role, helping to validate the model.

Bean and Metzner (1985, 1987) were the first to suggest that nontraditional students might intersect and be influenced by the college environment differently, compared to students at 4-year residential colleges. Although this study is not specific to community college students, nontraditional students, as Bean and Metzner (1985) define them, account for a significant proportion of community college students. As a seminal theoretical piece, their framework questioned previous assumptions about the homogeneity of college students and probed understanding of how the college environment affects students differently.

Model of Undergraduate Socialization.   Weidman's (1989) Model of Undergraduate Socialization incorporates both psychological and social-structural influences on student change (Pascarella & Terenzini, 2005). Although the model follows a similar linear structure as Astin's I-E-O model (1970a, 1970b), including student background, experiences, and outcomes, it diverges from I-E-O by focusing on the precollege, parental, and in-college normative pressures that shape and constrain student choices and growth (Pascarella & Terenzini, 2005).

Furthermore, Weidman (1989) "places great importance on continuing parental socialization, regardless of the students' proximity to the parents. He notes that college students are heavily influenced by their parents and this influence can override the authority of college faculty and the college student's peers" (Myers, 2008, p. 32). This feature is an aspect that positions this model both to be useful in a community college context and, simultaneously, to be problematic. First, unlike other models of college impact, Weidman hypothesizes the importance of noncollege influences and reference groups for students (Pascarella & Terenzini, 2005). This recognition of external factors on college impact is a critical element to include when attempting to understand the community college student experience. Yet, given the heavy representation of older than average and "nontraditional" students at this institution type, for many students at community colleges, the parental role and influence may be less relevant, as opposed to, for example, being a parent him- or herself.

A Theory of Student Persistence in Commuter Colleges and Universities. Most recently, Braxton, Hirschy, and McLendon (2014) proposed a theory of student persistence that is tailored to students at commuter colleges. They argue that (a) the theory of student departure (Tinto, 1975) lacks explanatory power for these institution types and (b) the important role of external communities and obligations for commuter students warrants a dedicated theory to help explain the impact of college on their persistence decisions (Braxton et al., 2014). The longitudinal model, like many of those reviewed thus far, begins with student entry characteristics and the students' initial institutional commitment. Next, students experience their external environment, campus environment, academic and intellectual development, and subsequent institutional commitment. Finally, the outcome of interest is persistence.

Braxton et al. (2014) tested their theory of student persistence in commuter colleges and universities using multivariate analysis and analytical cascading to identify significant influences on key dimension. They found that,

> the more a student perceives that their college or university is committed to the welfare of its students, the greater their degree of academic and intellectual development. Likewise, the greater the degree of academic and intellectual development perceived by a student, the greater their degree of subsequent commitment to (college). In addition, the more a student perceives that their college or university exhibits institutional integrity, the greater the student's degree of subsequent commitment to their college or university. In turn, the greater the subsequent commitment to the institution espoused by the student, the greater their likelihood of persistence in a commuter (college). (Braxton et al., 2014, p. 201)

Ultimately the test partially confirmed the theory, while leaving room for continued revisions.

This theory has promise as a useful tool for explaining the impact of college on the persistence of community colleges. Though similar to Bean and Metzner's (1985) model, although the focus on commuter students reflects a majority of community college students, it expands beyond this institutional type. Braxton et al.'s (2014) test may include but not be limited to community college students. Therefore, the applicability and explanatory power of the model for community college students remains to be explored.

Implications and Recommendations

The theories and models reviewed in this chapter are certainly not the only approaches to exploring the impact of college on important student outcomes, but they have been among the most enduring, frequently used, and relevant frameworks for examining college impact within community colleges. That said, historically the models were based on an assumption that all students in higher education are like 4-year, residential college students, but as college impact and student success research has evolved it has increasingly focused on more specific institution types and student populations. Yet, despite the creation of models that come close to addressing the community college context, they generally remain one degree removed. As a result, the use of these models as heuristics to better understand community colleges and their students is possible, but their applicability and alignment are questionable; therefore, there continues a need for more focused research on college impact at community colleges.

The challenge with the most longstanding and foundational models is the heavy focus on the on-campus and social elements of the environment, to the near exclusion of the external environment. Although the external environment is not strictly part of the "campus," when examining the impact of a community college on its students, the research has demonstrated that it is a required element. More recent revisions of Tinto's (2012) model and the frameworks that describe the experience of college students that are found at community colleges include or acknowledge the importance of external elements. Any future research or models related to college impact in community colleges must do the same.

Core to the future of the college impact literature in relation to community colleges is to have research and models that focus solely on this institution type. Although existing models involving nontraditional students (Bean & Metzner, 1985) and commuter students (Braxton et al., 2004, 2014) are relevant, they do not allow for a focused examination and recognition of the unique aspects of community colleges. Community colleges and their students have historically been underresearched; college impact is an area in which we can begin to remediate that oversight.

Community colleges are principal sites for issues of student success and implementation of best practices that support students' goals. The college impact literature and concepts have the potential to help practitioners make better program and policy decisions for their students; they can use the literature to examine and improve the effectiveness and impact that their institution has on its students. Yet, if they are not exposed to this literature they (a) are arguably less prepared to work in this institutional context and/or (b) may not be exposed to or using theoretical literature to inform and support program and policy creation and decision-making. To address this, two recommendations are provided. First, as stated previously, there need to be more community college specific literature and frameworks from which to draw. Second, assuming there is foundational literature available, it needs to be used in preparation and training programs. Latz and Royer (2014) found that in student affairs and higher education master's programs, the formal curriculum on community colleges is largely absent. This raises an issue about how accessible and useful conceptual literature that specifically draws together college impact and community colleges is if it is not part of the curriculum in preparation programs.

References

American Association of Community Colleges. (AACC; 2014). *Empowering community colleges: To build the nation's future–An implementation guide*. Washington, D.C.: Author. Retrieved from http://www.aacc21stcenturycenter.org/wp-content/uploads/2014/04/EmpoweringCommunityColleges_final.pdf

American Association of Community Colleges. (AACC; 2012). *The American graduate initiative: Stronger American skills through community colleges*. Washington, D.C.: Author. Retrieved from http://www.aacc.nche.edu/Advocacy/aginitiative/Documents/ccfactsheet.pdf

American Council on Education. (1937). *The student personnel point of view* (American Council on Education Studies, series 1, vol. 1, no. 3). Washington, DC: Author.

American Council on Education. (1949). *The student personnel point of view* (Rev. ed.). Washington, DC: Author.

Astin, A.W. (1970a). The methodology of research on college impact (I). *Sociology of Education*, 43, 223–254.

Astin, A. A.W.(1970b). The methodology of research on college impact (II). *Sociology of Education*, 43, 437–450.

Astin, A.W. (1975). *Preventing students from dropping out*. San Francisco: Jossey-Bass.

Astin, A. W. (1985). *Achieving educational excellence: A critical assessment of priorities and practices in higher education*. San Francisco: Jossey-Bass.

Astin, A. W.(1991). *Assessment for excellence: The philosophy and practice of assessment and evaluation in higher education*. New York: Macmillan.

Bean, J., & Metzner, B. (1985). A conceptual model of nontraditional undergraduate student attrition. *Review of Educational Research*, 55, 485–540.

Bean, J. P., & Metzner, B. S. (1987). The estimation of a conceptual model of nontraditional undergraduate student attrition. *Research in Higher Education*, 27(1), 15–36.

Braxton, J. M., Hirschy, A. S., & McClendon, S. A. (2004). Understanding and reducing college student departure. ASHE-ERIC Higher Education Report, Volume 30, Number 3 (Vol. 16). San Francisco: Jossey-Bass.

Braxton, J.M., Doyle, W.R., Hartley III, H.V., Hirschy, A.S., Jones, W.A., & McLendon, M.K. (2014). *Rethinking college student retention*. San Francisco: Jossey-Bass.

Cabrera, A. F., Castaneda, M.B., Nora, A., & Hengstler, D. (1992). The convergence between two theories of college persistence. *Journal of Higher Education*, 63(2), 143–164.

Deegan, W. L., & O'Banion, T. (1989). Editors' notes. *New Directions for Community Colleges: No. 67. Perspectives on student development*, (pp. 1–3). San Francisco: Jossey-Bass.

Helfgot, S., & Culp, M. (2005). Editors' Notes. *New Directions for Community Colleges: No. 131. Community college student affairs: What really matters* (pp. 1–4). San Francisco: Jossey-Bass.

Latz, A. O., & Royer, D. W. (2014, April). *Master's-level student affairs preparation programs and community college courses: Surveying the landscape*. Paper presentation given at the Council for the Study of Community Colleges Annual Conference, Washington, D.C.

Myers, L.C. (2008). *Student success in an urban community college: Applying the expertise model of student success*. Retrieved from Proquest.

Napoli, A. R., & Wortman, P. M. (1996). A meta-analysis of the impact of academic and social integration on persistence of community college students. *Journal of Applied Research in the Community College, 4*, 5–21.

Napoli, A. R., & Wortman, P. M. (1998). Psychosocial factors related to retention and early departure of two-year community college students. *Research in Higher Education, 39*(4), 419–451.

Obama, B. (2009). Remarks of President Barack Obama—As Prepared for Delivery Address to Joint Session of Congress. Retrieved on 3/17/09 from http://www.whitehouse.gov/the_press_office/remarks-of-president-barack-obama-address-to-joint-session-of-congress/.

Pascarella, E.T., & Terenzini, P.T. (2005). *How college effects students. Vol. 2. A third decade of research.* San Francisco: Jossey-Bass.

Rendon, L., Jalomo, R., & Nora, A. (2000). Theoretical considerations in the study of minority student retention in higher education. In J. Braxton (Ed.), *Rethinking ing the departure puzzle: New theory and research on college student retention* (pp. 127–156). Nashville, TN: Vanderbilt University Press.

Tierney, W. (2000). Power, identity, and the dilemma of college student departure. In J. Braxton (Ed.), *Reworking the student departure puzzle* (pp. 213–234). Nashville, TN: Vanderbilt University Press.

Tinto, V. (1975). Dropout from higher education: A theoretical synthesis of recent research. *Review of Educational Research, 45*, 213–125.

Tinto, V. (1987). *Leaving college: Rethinking the causes and cures of student attrition.* Chicago: University of Chicago Press.

Tinto, V. (1993). *Leaving college: Rethinking the causes and cures of student attrition* (2nd ed.). Chicago, IL: Univeristy of Chicago Press.

Tinto, V. (2012). *Completing college: Rethinking institutional action.* Chicago, IL: University of Chicago Press.

Weidman, J. (1989). Undergraduate socialization: A conceptual approach. In J. Smart (Ed.), *Higher education: Handbook of theory and research* (Vol. 5, pp. 289–322). New York: Agathon.

C. CASEY OZAKI is an Associate Professor in Teaching and Learning at the University of North Dakota. She received her Ph.D. in Higher Education from Michigan State University.

NEW DIRECTIONS FOR COMMUNITY COLLEGES • DOI: 10.1002/cc

3

The authors of this chapter present the Socio-Ecological Outcomes Model as a means of predicting student success for community college men of color.

Applying the Socio-Ecological Outcomes Model to the Student Experiences of Men of Color

Frank Harris III, J. Luke Wood

For nearly two decades, there has been a proliferation of attention among scholars, educational leaders, and policymakers about postsecondary access and success for men of color. Although most of this attention has been directed toward Black and Latino men enrolled at 4-year institutions where attrition rates among these men are alarmingly high, stakeholders have begun to raise questions about men of color who enroll at 2-year institutions. The concern about men of color at 2-year institutions has been fueled, in part, by the recognition that community colleges serve the overwhelming majority of men of color who participate in postsecondary education. In our home state of California, for example, 82% of Black, 81% of Latino, 79% of Native American, and 68% of Filipino men who were enrolled in public postsecondary education in 2010 attended community colleges (California Postsecondary Education Commission, 2011).

Despite the heavy concentration of men of color in community colleges, theoretical and conceptual models that explain their development and success have been virtually absent from the published scholarship. Consequently, both scholars and practitioners have relied heavily on student success models that prioritize 4-year institutional contexts and overlook race/ethnicity, gender, and other salient pieces in the student success puzzle for men of color in community colleges. In an effort to address this gap in the body of work on men of color in community colleges, in this chapter, we propose the Socio-Ecological Outcomes (SEO) Model. The SEO model accounts for the primary factors affecting the success of men of color in community colleges, highlighting interactions between societal, environmental, intrapersonal, and campus-based factors that influence

NEW DIRECTIONS FOR COMMUNITY COLLEGES, no. 174, Summer 2016 © 2016 Wiley Periodicals, Inc.
Published online in Wiley Online Library (wileyonlinelibrary.com) • DOI: 10.1002/cc.20201

student success outcomes for these men. We offer this model as a framework to inform educational research and practice on this population. In the next section of this chapter, we discuss the background and development of the SEO model and its key constructs. After that, we discuss interactions among the key constructs. We conclude the chapter with a brief discussion of practical implications of the model.

Background and Development of the SEO Model

The SEO emerged from *The Five Domains: A Conceptual Model of Black Male Success in Community Colleges* (Wood & Harris, in press). The five domains model focuses exclusively on Black male student success in community colleges and was based on an interdisciplinary synthesis of relevant literature and research on the experiences of Black men in postsecondary education, community college student success, Black masculinity, and Black identity development. Based on our review and synthesis of this work, we identified five factors that have been prioritized in scholarly discussions of the experiences and outcomes of Black men in community colleges: social factors, noncognitive factors, academic factors, environmental factors, and institutional factors. Our examination of these factors, interactions among them, and their impact on academic success for Black men in community colleges led to the development of the *Five Domains* model.

Although the five domains model is the precursor to the SEO model, it differs in two notable respects. First, the SEO model has broader application in that it accounts for the experiences and outcomes of men of color (e.g., Black, Latino, Native American, and Southeast Asian), whereas the five domains model focuses exclusively on Black men. Second, in addition to being informed by the published literature and research on men of color, the SEO model has been field tested and is grounded empirically by initial findings from the Community College Survey of Men (CCSM)—a comprehensive needs assessment instrument that has been completed by nearly 4,000 male community college students across 27 colleges. As a result, the SEO model is more parsimonious than its predecessor in that it is composed of the most salient factors that are known to influence student success outcomes for men of color in community colleges and is a more accurate portrayal of the relationships and interactions between these factors.

In addition to aforementioned literature and research on student success for men of color in community colleges, the SEO model is also informed by Astin's (1993) Input-Environment-Outputs (IEO) model. Astin proposed the IEO model to account for input variables or prior educational experiences and characteristics that students bring to the educational environment. By doing so, educators are better able to measure how educational variables affect student outcomes. According to Astin, "inputs" are the personal qualities and characteristics students bring to an educational program, the "environment" includes students' actual experiences during the educational program, and "outputs" are the "talents" educators hope students develop by way of their involvement in the program (p. 18). Although the constructs of the SEO model are not completely analogous to the constructs of the IEO model, there are some clear similarities between the two.

Key Constructs of the SEO Model

As shown in Figure 3.1, the SEO model is composed of seven key constructs, each of which is depicted in rectangular boxes.

Inputs. The first two constructs in the SEO model—*background/ defining and societal factors*—are described as "inputs" in that they account for the factors and experiences that occur for men of color prior to matriculation to community college. These factors influence their success. Both students and educators have little control over these factors; yet, they can have an observable impact on student success for men of color if they are ignored or not taken into account in educational programming and service delivery. Student demographics (e.g., age, citizenship status, primary language), enrollment status (e.g., part-time, full-time), and levels of academic preparation are considered background/defining factors in the SEO model. A host of background/defining factors are consistently noted in the published scholarship as having a significant influence on student success outcomes for men of color, notably their age (Hagedorn, Maxwell, &

Figure 3.1.   Socio-Ecological Outcomes (SEO) Model

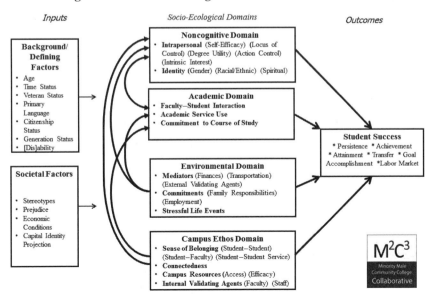

Hampton, 2001), educational goals (Mason, 1998), and academic preparation (Hagedorn et al., 2001; Perrakis, 2008). Societal factors are also depicted as inputs in the SEO model. This factor captures the larger sociocultural forces that lead men of color to community colleges and the internalized societal messages that shape perceptions of men of color. For example, it is widely documented that most men of color who participate in postsecondary education are enrolled at a community college and a critical mass of those who attend 4-year institutions began at a community college (Beginning Postsecondary Students, 2009). The myriad of reasons men of color are disproportionately represented in community colleges (when compared to those who are enrolled at 4-year institutions) cannot be adequately accounted for in one model. However, some reasons may be economic in nature, whereas others may be attributed to the accessibility of community colleges. Racist stereotypes and prejudices about men of color, including academic inferiority, negative dispositions toward education, athletic prowess, and even criminal behavior, can lead educators and even men of color themselves to question the extent to which they belong and can succeed in community college (Bush, Bush, & Wilcoxson, 2009; Harper, 2009; Wood & Turner, 2010).

Socio-ecological Domains.   The four rectangular boxes positioned in the middle of the model represent its core and account for the experiences and interactions occurring subsequent to the matriculation of men of color to community colleges. These are factors that influence their success. Consistent with the language we used in our presentation of the five domains model (Wood & Harris, in press), each of these domains is presented in the model as discrete spheres of activity, and relationships and interactions among them are fluid and dynamic. Moreover, we described these domains as "socio-ecological" because they capture the interplay between salient sociological and environmental factors that interact and shape student success outcomes for men of color in community colleges. These domains include the noncognitive domain, the academic domain, the environmental domain, and the campus ethos domain.

The *noncognitive domain* is composed of variables that are primarily psychosocial and captures students' emotional and affective responses to social contexts and the person–environment interactions that take place within the institution. Intrapersonal factors, or those that are situated within the individual, are also important noncognitive considerations that influence student success outcomes for men of color. For instance, the extent to which students believe they are capable of being successful in college (self-efficacy), the amount of personal control they assume they have for their success (locus of control), the value they place on obtaining a college degree or certificate (degree utility), and the energy and focus they invest toward their academic endeavors (action control) all come into play in shaping student success outcomes for men of color.

With regard to identity, given the SEO's model's focus on men of color, the interaction between race/ethnicity and gender, notably masculinity, must also be acknowledged. For men of color, the intersection between race and gender can complicate their college experiences in unique ways. Harris and Harper (2008) noted that men are socialized to view school settings as feminine spaces and, thus, may view academic activities like studying and participating in class as contradictory to the values they have learned to associate with masculinity. The conflict between masculinity and schooling can be experienced intensely for men from low-income underserved backgrounds who often feel pressure to fulfill the role of breadwinner in their homes. Thus, sacrificing earnings in order to attend school can be a difficult decision for these students.

The salience of racial/ethnic and gender identity in the experiences and outcomes of men of color in community colleges is reported in several key studies. For example, Gardenhire-Crooks et al. (2010) and Sutherland (2011) attributed negative experiences and interactions men of color reported having with faculty and administrators to judgments they made about these students based on their appearances (e.g., baggy clothes, tattoos, braided hair). Wood and Essien-Wood (2012) and Gardenhire-Crooks et al. (2010) also noted how internalized identity conflicts served as barriers to success in community college. Gardenhire-Crooks et al. (2010) found that for men of color, socialization as "breadwinners" led them to prioritize work and earning money over their engagement in academic endeavors. Wood and Essien-Wood (2012) found that men of color who embraced capitalistic values and measured their self-worth by their ability to acquire material wealth and possessions were likely to experience negative outcomes in community college.

The *academic domain* consists of student interactions with faculty, student use of academic services, their commitment to their course of study, and other variables that are directly related to student academic experiences and outcomes. The interactions of students with faculty have been widely considered in the recent research on men of color in community colleges (e.g., Bush, Bush, & Wilcoxson 2009; Flowers, 2006; Wood, 2012; Wood & Turner, 2010). Generally, this research has concluded that although these interactions are integral to the success of men of color, they are reluctant to pursue faculty interaction because they have the perception that faculty are unsupportive and uncaring. The use of academic services such as tutoring and academic advising by men of color, (Glenn, 2003; Mason, 1998), and the extent to which they are committed to a course of study (Hagedorn et al., 2001; Mason, 1998), have also been identified as key variables within the academic domain that influences men of color and their success in community college.

The *environmental domain* of the SEO model captures important student commitments that occur outside of the institution. These commitments may direct the time, attention, and other resources of men of color away from their academic pursuits. External commitments that have been identified as especially salient among men of color are family responsibilities and employment (Mason, 1998). Stressful life events, such as a divorce, death in the family, eviction/homelessness, or job loss, are also situated in the environmental domain because they have been identified by scholars as having a negative impact on persistence in community college (Freeman & Huggans, 2009; Wood & Williams, 2013). Although external commitments and stressful life events are believed to negatively influence the success of men of color in community college, these commitments and events can be mediated by targeted support. For example, financial resources (e.g., grants, scholarships, book vouchers) that reduce the need to work full time off campus and transportation resources that reduce commuting time and make it easier for students to get to and from campus, can mediate the negative effects that external commitments may have on engagement and success in college for men of color.

Validating agents outside of campus who provide encouragement and support to students, especially during challenging times, are also important external mediators that can counteract the negative effects of environmental commitments. Rendón (1994) described validation as "an enabling, confirming, and supportive process initiated by in- and out-of-class agents to foster academic and interpersonal development" (p. 44). Rendón argued that validating agents are especially critical for college persistence and success for *nontraditional students*, as they often have doubts about their abilities to be successful in college. Nontraditional students include those from low-income backgrounds, historically underrepresented and underserved students, and students who are financially independent.

In the SEO model, we distinguish internal and external validating agents. Internal validating agents (which are situated in the campus ethos domain and discussed later in this chapter) are faculty, administrators, and student services professionals who help students navigate the institution, teach them how to access campus resources, and provide information to help them succeed in college. Conversely, external validating agents can be significant others, family members, friends, and other individuals in students' lives who provide encouragement and the support necessary for students to be successful in college. External validation was described as "outside encouragement" in the persistence model for African American male urban community college students proposed by Mason (1998). According to Mason, "the more support the student had received from outside the college (this was generally found to be from a significant female—mother, girlfriend, wife), the more likely the student was to persist" (p. 758). For example, a family member who provides childcare while a student attends classes, a boss who allows a student to adjust his work schedule to allow for ample study time or a partner who offers messages of praise and encouragement are examples of external validating agents. Given the pull effect that environmental factors can have on student success (or lack thereof) in community college, external validation is prioritized and shown as a mediator in the environmental domain of the SEO model.

In the *campus ethos* domain, institutional policies, programs, campus resources, and day-to-day practices that shape the way students experience and succeed in community college are presented. Many traditional models of student success place the onus for student success solely on students and disregard the role that institutional leaders and educators play in facilitating success. The SEO model underscores the institution's responsibility in fostering a culture that is conducive to learning and success for men of color and situate the factors that are necessary to do so in the campus ethos domain. Our conceptualization of student success is informed by Bensimon's (2007) concepts of equity-mindedness and institutional responsibility. According to Bensimon, equity-minded practitioners (e.g., faculty, administrators, student services professionals) attribute outcome disparities to "institution-based dysfunctions" rather than student deficits (p. 446). Thus, when outcome inequities are viewed this way, practitioners are more likely to seek and apply strategies that focus on fixing the institution or adjusting their own practices rather than rely exclusively on strategies to remediate perceived student deficits.

Consistent with Bensimon's (2007) conceptualization, internal validating agents are positioned in the campus ethos domain of the SEO model because of the critical role they play in making campus environments more welcoming and affirming for students. Recall in our earlier discussion of Rendón's (1994) concept of validation, internal validating agents are faculty, student services staff, and even peers who support students by sharing important information, facilitating access to campus resources, eliminating structural barriers that impede student success, and communicating messages of encouragement and self determination to students. This can be especially important for men of color who may have had invalidating educational experiences and relationships throughout their schooling.

A sense of belonging and connectedness for students to the campus are also key variables in the campus ethos domain. According to Hurtado and Carter (1997), sense of belonging is a concept that "captures the individual's view of whether he or she feels included in the college community" (p. 327). Furthermore, they argued that student persistence and success in college is predicated on the extent to which students perceive the institutional environment as welcoming. Finally, Hurtado and Carter concluded that student perceptions of the campus racial climate are a salient factor for Latino students' success. To varying degrees, findings from Perrakis (2008), Gardenhire-Crooks et al. (2010), Sutherland (2011), and Wood and Turner (2010) speak to why a sense of belonging and connectedness to the campus are factors that influences student success for men of color in community colleges. Findings from these studies confirm that perceiving the campus as accepting and affirming is paramount to men of color's willingness to engage, seek help, and establish authentic relationships with faculty, student services professionals, and other students.

Campus resources that facilitate student success in college (e.g., academic advising, career counseling, transfer services, computer labs, tutoring) are also situated in the campus ethos domain of the SEO model. Findings and insights that have emerged from our research on the experiences of men of color in community colleges confirm that campus resources need not only be available but also accessible and efficacious in order for them to have a desired impact on student success for men of color. Institutional barriers that make key resources difficult to access will reduce the likelihood that men of color will seek them. For example, if the institution is not offering academic advising at a convenient time of the day, or academic advising is accessible only in person, then students may not use that service, regardless of how helpful advising may be. As for the efficacy of campus resources, once students have the opportunity to access them, they must see them as making a positive difference in their college experiences and having a meaningful impact on their success. The accessibility and efficacy of campus resources are especially important for men of color because the social construction of masculinity encourages men to embrace an attitude of independence and to avoid vulnerability or admit weaknesses. This often results in a negative disposition toward help-seeking (Harris & Harper, 2008) and a reluctance among men to use campus support services. For example, men of color in Gardenhire-Crooks et al.'s (2010) study reported being reluctant to seek help with personal, academic and financial problems because they perceived doing so as a threat to their masculinity.

Outcomes.   The outcomes variable of the SEO model is positioned at the far right. Essentially, we contend that dynamic and interdependent relationships among the key constructs of the SEO model, which take into account the sociocultural experiences and backgrounds that men of color bring with them to community college as well as the experiences and interactions that take place within the socio-ecological domains, shape student success outcomes for these students in meaningful and observable ways. As such, persistence, degree and certificate attainment, achievement as measured by grade point average, transfer, and other student goals are the result of the constructs and interactions that are depicted in the model.

Interactions Among Key Constructs of the SEO Model

The SEO model shows that each domain (i.e., noncognitive, academic, environmental, campus ethos) influences student success (e.g., persistence, achievement, attainment, transfer). However, like all social phenomena, the experiences of men of color in community colleges do not occur in isolated domains. As such, the SEO model recognizes interactive relationships between the variable domains. Five key interactive relationships are depicted in the model and discussed in this section of the chapter.

First, the campus ethos domain has an effect on the academic domain. For example, the model suggests that students' feeling of belonging and connectedness to the campus and its affiliates influences their interactions with faculty and use of campus services. Specifically, greater feelings of connectedness and belonging are associated with greater and more authentic interactions with faculty and use of academic services that are designed to enhance student success.

Second, the campus ethos domain is also seen as influencing the noncognitive domain. For instance, when students receive validation from faculty and staff, they may experience greater feelings of confidence in academic matters (self-efficacy) and can begin to internalize the worthwhileness of pursuing a college degree (degree utility). Moreover, healthy campus environments are also seen as being essential to students' identity development. For example, as noted by Harris, Palmer, and Struve (2011) campus climates that are rife with stereotypes and racism intensify negative concepts of masculinity.

Third, the environmental domain is also seen as influencing the noncognitive domain. Take for example work and family obligations; the greater a student's commitment in these areas, the more they can detract from their focus in college (action control) and conflict with their ability to reap intrinsic rewards (intrinsic interest) from their studies.

Fourth, the environmental domain interacts with the academic domain in a manner similar to its interaction with the noncognitive domain. Environmental factors (e.g., stressful life events, limited financial resources, transportation challenges) can pull students away from relationships with faculty, inhibit their ability to use campus services, and detract from their commitment to academic pursuits. The influence of the environmental domain on the academic and noncognitive domains is particularly salient, given that many institutions struggle to address external challenges in students' lives. For example, colleges may often balk at addressing environmental challenges because (a) they occur external to the institution and are perceived as outside of the institution's locus of control; and (b) they typically require a substantial investment of institutional resources (e.g., scholarships, bus passes, on-campus childcare, free textbooks). However, based on the SEO model, the environmental domain largely has an effect on student success through the academic and noncognitive domains, both of which are within an institution's locus of control.

Finally, the authors of the SEO model recognize the interplay between the academic domain and the noncognitive domain, suggesting there is a mutual, bidirectional exchange between the two. For instance, faculty–student interactions can shape a student's self-efficacy and perceptions of the utility of college. However, self-efficacy and degree utility can then shape future interactions with other faculty members. The same can be said for the effect of academic service use on these intrapersonal factors.

Conclusion

Given that the SEO model is informed by the published scholarship on men of color in community colleges and from data that were collected from nearly 4,000 male community college students, its application in practice and future research studies of this population is potentially far-reaching. Fully unpacking how the model can be applied is beyond the scope and purpose of this chapter. However, we encourage educators who are positioned to facilitate the success of men of color by way of teaching, designing programs, delivering student services, and developing institutional policies, to consider the key constructs and interactions that are presented in the model. Colleges that rely on minority male initiatives to enable student success will also likely find the SEO model useful in informing these interventions. At a minimum, these constructs should be the basis of campus-based assessment efforts. The CCSM and the Community College Student Success Inventory (see Harris & Wood, 2014; Wood & Harris, 2013) are two campus-based assessment tools we have developed that are aligned with the SEO model. The SEO model can also inform professional development and other efforts to build practitioners' capacities to serve men of color responsibly and equitably. Finally, beyond the practical implications of the SEO model, scholars who study the experiences and outcomes of men of color should also consider it in future inquiries on this population.

References

Astin, A. W. (1993). *What matters in college? Four critical years revisited.* San Francisco, CA: Jossey-Bass.

Beginning Postsecondary Students. (2009). *Reason enrolled 2004 to transfer to four year college (yes) by community college student 6-year retention and attainment 2009, for race/ethnicity. Beginning Postsecondary Students Longitudinal Study.* Washington, DC: National Center for Education Statistics.

Bensimon, E. M. (2007). The underestimated significance of practitioner knowledge in the scholarship of student success. *Review of Higher Education, 30,* 441–469.

Bush, E. C., Bush, L., & Wilcoxson, D. (2009). One initiative at a time: A look at emerging African American male programs in the California community college system. In H. T. Frierson, W. Pearson, Jr., & J. H. Wyche (Eds.), *Black American males in higher education: Diminishing proportions* (pp. 253–270). Bingley, UK: Emerald Group.

California Postsecondary Education Commission (2011). *Proportion of men of color enrolled in California's public postsecondary institutions.* Sacramento, CA: California Postsecondary Education Commission.

Flowers, L. A. (2006). Effects of attending a two-year institution on African American males' academic and social integration in the first year of college. *Teachers College Record, 108,* 267–286.

Freeman, T. L., & Huggans, M. A. (2009). Persistence of African-American male community college students in engineering. In H. T. Frierson, W. Pearson, Jr., &

NEW DIRECTIONS FOR COMMUNITY COLLEGES • DOI: 10.1002/cc

J. H. Wyche (Eds.), *Black American males in higher education: Diminishing proportions* (pp. 229–251). Bingley, UK: Emerald Group.

Gardenhire-Crooks, A., Collado, H., Martin, K., Castro, A., Brock, T., & Orr, G. (2010). *Terms of engagement: Men of color discuss their experiences in community college.* New York, NY: MDRC.

Glenn, F. S. (2003). The retention of Black male students in Texas public community colleges. *Journal of College Student Retention, 5,* 115–133.

Hagedorn, L. S., Maxwell, W., & Hampton, P. (2001). Correlates of retention for African-American males in the community college. *Journal of College Student Retention, 3,* 243–263.

Harper, S. R. (2009). Race, interest convergence, and transfer outcomes for Black male student athletes. In L. S. Hagedorn & D. Horton, Jr., *New Directions for Community Colleges: No. 147. Student athletes and athletics* (pp. 29–37). San Francisco, CA: Jossey-Bass.

Harris, F., III, & Harper, S. R. (2008). Masculinities go to community college: Understanding male identity socialization and gender role conflict. In J. Lester (Ed.), *New Directions for Community Colleges: No. 142. Gendered perspectives on community colleges* (pp. 25–35). San Francisco, CA: Jossey-Bass.

Harris, F., III., Palmer, R. T., & Struve, L. E. (2011). "Cool posing" on campus: A qualitative study of masculinities and gender expression among Black men at a private research institution. *Journal of Negro Education, 80*(1), 47–62.

Harris, F., III., & Wood, J. L. (2014). Community college student success inventory (CCSSI) for men of color in community colleges: Content validation summary. *Community College Journal of Research and Practice, 38*(12), 1185–1192.

Hurtado, S., & Carter, D. F. (1997). Effects of college transition and perceptions of the campus racial climate on Latino students' sense of belonging. *Sociology of Education, 70,* 324–345.

Mason, H. P. (1998). A persistence model for African American male urban community college students. *Community College Journal of Research and Practice, 22,* 751–760.

Perrakis, A. I. (2008). Factors promoting academic success among African American and White male community college students. In J. Lester (Ed.), *New Directions for Community Colleges: No. 142. Gendered perspectives on community colleges* (pp. 15–23). San Francisco, CA: Jossey-Bass.

Rendón, L. I. (1994). Validating culturally diverse students: Toward a new model of learning and student development. *Innovative Higher Education, 19*(1), 33–51.

Sutherland, J. A. (2011). Building an academic nation through social networks: Black immigrant men in community colleges. *Community College Journal of Research and Practice, 35,* 267–279.

Wood, J. L. (2012). Black males in the community college: Using two national datasets to examine academic and social integration. *Journal of Black Masculinity, 2,* 56–88.

Wood, J. L., & Essien-Wood, I. R. (2012). Capital identity projection: Understanding the psychosocial effects of capitalism on Black male community college students. *Journal of Economic Psychology, 33,* 984–995.

Wood, J. L., & Harris, F., III. (2013). The Community College Survey of Men: An initial validation of the instrument's non-cognitive outcomes construct. *Community College Journal of Research and Practice, 37,* 333–338.

Wood, J. L., & Harris, F., III. (in press). The "five domains": A conceptual model of Black male success in the community college. In F. Bonner (Ed.), *Frameworks and models of Black male success: A guide for P–12 and postsecondary educators.* Sterling, VA: Stylus.

Wood, J. L., & Turner, C. S. V. (2010). Black males and the community college: Student perspectives on faculty and academic success. *Community College Journal of Research and Practice, 35,* 135–151.

Wood, J. L., & Williams, R. C. (2013). Persistence factors for Black males in the community college: An examination of background, academic, social, and environmental variables. *Spectrum, 1*(2), 1–28.

FRANK HARRIS III *is an associate professor in postsecondary education at San Diego State University. He received his Ed.D in Higher Education from the University of Southern California Rossier School of Education.*

J. LUKE WOOD *is associate professor of community college leadership at San Diego State University. He received a Ph.D in Educational Leadership and Policy Studies at Arizona State University.*

4

This chapter details the perspectives of LGBTQ collegians and faculty/staff allies at 2-year institutions.

Tracing LGBTQ Community College Students' Experiences

Eboni M. Zamani-Gallaher, Devika Dibya Choudhuri

The 2-year college sector has long been the tier of higher education that embraces access to underserved and underrepresented students enrolling a significant share of first-generation, female, low-income, racially/ethnically diverse students, single parents, and students with disabilities. Community colleges enroll 46% of all U.S. undergraduates (American Association of Community Colleges, 2015). Among community college students, 36% are first generation, 57% are female, 33% are eligible for Pell grants, 16% qualify for federal work-study, and 21% qualify for federal supplemental educational opportunity grants. Students of color comprise 45% (14% African American, 21% Hispanic, 6% Asian/Pacific Islander, 1% Native American, 3% bi/multiracial) of those attending community colleges, 2-year institutions enroll 17% of single parents, and 12% of community college students are persons with disabilities (American Association of Community Colleges, 2015). Although the literature on underrepresented, underserved, marginalized students in 2- and 4-year colleges arguably calls for additional examination, little is known about LGBTQ (lesbian, gay, bisexual, transgender, and queer) students at community colleges.

A Needle in a Haystack: LGBTQ Students in Community Colleges Literature

With more than two-fifths of undergraduates attending 2-year institutions, greater emphasis and disciplined study on the diversity within diverse groups are needed. More specifically, studies that extend our understanding of the collegiate experiences of LGBTQ learners on community college campuses would contribute greatly to the field. A majority of the

NEW DIRECTIONS FOR COMMUNITY COLLEGES, no. 174, Summer 2016 © 2016 Wiley Periodicals, Inc.
Published online in Wiley Online Library (wileyonlinelibrary.com) • DOI: 10.1002/cc.20202

literature on LGBTQ students takes place in the 4-year institutional context and describes theoretical and developmental models developed using traditional-aged, racially homogeneous, 4-year college students. A dearth of publications considers the community college context for LGBTQ students (Garvey, Taylor, & Rankin, 2015; Ivory, 2005; Sanlo & Espinoza, 2012). The few writings that have sought to center community college LGBTQ students in the discourse, offer synthesis and critique of existing studies that largely focus on LGBTQ students, policies, and practices at 4-year colleges and universities.

Franklin (1998) investigated homophobia among community college students. Although perceptions and attitudes toward LGBTQ students were measured, the core of the study sought understanding the psychology behind motivations for hate crimes that used a community college sample. In short, LGBTQ 2-year collegians were not the focal point of Franklin's inquiry. Also of note is the inattention to in-class experiences and fostering inclusive class environments for LGBTQ students in community colleges. Recently, Garvey, Taylor, & Rankin (2015) conducted a comparison of LGBTQ student classroom experiences in 2- and 4-year institutions of higher learning. Overall, results from the authors' mixed-methods study found community college LGBTQ students reported greater use of heterosexist language and chilly campus climates.

Several researchers have added to the knowledge base on LGBTQ students with respect to identity development, coming out, and collegiate experiences (Cass, 1979; D'Augelli, 1994). There is breadth and depth in the extant literature documenting various patterns of student development, personal development, the process of coming out and self-actualization for LGBTQ college students. Furthermore, multiple studies have examined the college environment, creating safe zones, resources, programs, and services necessary to support LGBTQ students that foster retention, persistence, and collegiate satisfaction (Preston & Hoffman, 2015; Renn, 2010; Sanlo & Espinoza, 2012). Nonetheless, the aforementioned studies on coming out, intersections of identity, and campus climate largely do not take LGBTQ community college students or 2-year institutions into account, raising the question of whether or not they accurately and appropriately describe the experiences of students at community colleges.

Purpose of the Study

According to Ivory (2005), "Due to the invisible nature of the LGBTQ undergraduate population, it is difficult for student affairs professionals at community colleges to identify and address the needs of sexual minority students on campus" (p. 482). In the field of higher education, community colleges are often on the margins of the discourse regarding trends, educational climate, and experiences of 2-year collegians. Likewise, the voices and stories of people of color, women, persons with disabilities, low-income people, and so forth have traditionally been on the margins of published research; that which has been done has largely focused on the 4-year, not the 2-year sector. What is missing from the research is a distinct view of the everyday life of LGBTQ people attending community colleges. This exploratory study, emergent in nature was guided by the following research questions:

1. What are the coming-out experiences of community college LGBTQ students?
2. Are student support services for LGBTQ students at community colleges considered adequate?
3. Do LGBTQ students and faculty/staff allies perceive the community college climate as welcoming?

Given the aims of this study, intersectionality has conceptual underpinnings for the study as it allows for examination of oppressive systems and intersections between disenfranchised groups or minoritized groups (e.g., race, ethnicity, gender, sexual orientation, social class, etc.). Components of intersectionality most applicable to our study are vectors of privilege and oppression that may influence the lived experiences of LGBTQ community college students.

Methods

This study used a qualitative approach to explore the identities and experiences of LGBTQ students in community college settings. Given the complex nature of sexual orientation identity among community college students and the low level of empirical attention to this topic, a qualitative method was deemed particularly appropriate. Narrative research methods were applied in the current study, as it is particularly useful for exploratory studies, because narratives allow participants' voices to be heard and their lived experience to be analyzed.

Creswell (1994) contends a phenomenological approach is an orienting framework that seeks to centralize meaning about lived experience from those who live it. In the case of LGBTQ students in community colleges, we sought to understand their experiences through a multiplicity of perspectives. We used intersectionality as a guiding frame to acknowledge and make visible how multiple social identities manifest and negotiate across power relations. Although we centered our focus on sexual minority experiences, other aspects of identity were important, informing us regarding the context and expanding the ways in which we understood our participants. We appreciate that research is not atheoretical in nature and that knowledge is theory laden, as are methods. Hence, the role of theory in this qualitative study as presented earlier reflects guiding frameworks that illustrate ontological and epistemological relevance; however, it does not rely

New Directions for Community Colleges • DOI: 10.1002/cc

on a scaffolding framework of theory to constrain our findings. In sum, we find that in order to give agency, expression, and voice, qualitative research approaches are well suited for research exploring the experiences of marginalized groups such as LGBTQ students at community colleges.

Sampling and Participants.   Participants were recruited for the study using purposeful sampling techniques. E-mails were sent to student organizations and identified LGBTQ centers or allies at various community colleges, as well as snowball sampling from one participant to another, requesting time from participants for interviews. Interviews were conducted in person or by phone with 11 students (see Table 4.1) and 7 faculty/staff allies, 3 of whom were advisors for Gay-Straight Alliance student clubs (see Table 4.2). The participants represent five different colleges. Student participants were offered a small gift card for Amazon.com or Starbucks Coffee to express appreciation for their time. Participants were approached to do member checks on transcripts as well as to invite feedback. All interviews lasted 1 hour or more and all were audio-recorded.

Table 4.1   LGBTQ Community College Student Participants

Student Participant	Racial/Ethnic Self-Identification	Gender Self-Identification	Sexual Orientation
William	Black	Male	Gay
Arthur	White	Male	Gay
Alex	White	Female	Lesbian
Lisa	African American	Female	Lesbian
Matt	Jewish	*Transgender FTM	?
Colin	White	Male	Gay
Ray	Black	Male	Gay
Bristol	Caucasian	Female	Bisexual
Ben	White	Male	Gay
JB	White	Female	Bisexual
Monroe	White	Male	Gay

*Transgender FTM = Female to Male.

Table 4.2   Community College Faculty/Staff LGBTQ Allies

Employee Group	Participant Characteristics	Two-Year Institutional-Type
1-Faculty	Plus 50, White, Lesbian, Female	Single campus
1-Faculty	Middle-Aged White Lesbian, Female	Multicampus
3-Support Staff	1 White Female Bisexual	Single campus
	1 White Female Heterosexual	
	1 White Male Bisexual	
2-Administrators	1 Black Female; Sexuality Unknown	Multicampus
	1 White, Gender Nonconforming, Sexuality Unknown	

Data Analysis. We employed narrative thematic analysis underscoring what participants said as opposed to how they said it. Our analysis reflects word-for-word transcription of each interview and focus group. The first analysis stage involved generating open descriptive codes in the transcripts, followed by axial coding, clustering codes under broader categories. Then clusters were grouped into units of meaning that explicated some aspect of experience that seemed significant or relevant. Finally, overall themes emerged that were then explored by returning to the actual transcript and reading for the theme.

Trustworthiness. The trustworthiness of the findings was ensured through several safeguards. A triangulation process was invoked by involving multiple researchers who included the principal investigators as well as two graduate research assistants. In addition, early on, the investigators developed a set of questions to guide the interview process, and both investigators were present at early interviews making sure that we were asking from similar perspectives. We both reviewed transcripts of the interviews separately and together. We also continued to discuss the process of both data collection and interviewing collaboratively.

Findings

Students were between the ages of 18 and 26. Interestingly, only one of the 11 students was over 25 years old, which is not reflective of a student population that skews older. Each of the LGBTQ students in this study expressed educational aspirations beyond associate degrees. Several themes emerged, including the coming-out process, the significance of family, importance of religious messages, friends and support systems, as well as the challenges and goals of building systemic support for LGBTQ issues on community college campuses. Perhaps the most interesting and relevant was the separation of sexual orientation identity and experience and expectation of 2-year institutions.

All of the student participants came out while in high school, and many came to an understanding of themselves by sophomore or junior year, except for the transgender participant for whom the process was more complicated. Yet, their identity seemed silenced during their community college experience, or at the least largely unexpressed. Although hostile environments can create this underground experience, there was a host of other reasons that were addressed by student participants, administrators, and faculty advisors.

Desiring Inclusion, Finding, and Sustaining Community. Although sexual orientation identity was often described as holistic of who participants were (i.e., indistinguishable from themselves), their decision making about attending or choosing the community college seemed completely unrelated. They chose to attend community college for reasons related to preparation, career, and furthering goals but not because they expected support, much less active encouragement, from the environment. These restricted expectations were echoed and paralleled in the community college environments despite the best efforts of a few hardworking and dedicated faculty, staff, and administrators. One educator admitted, *"there's been a history of how we serve the students in terms of cocurricular stuff that's been very choppy … there wasn't a support mechanism.* As Matt said, *"the very transient nature of everyone here"* meant that it was hard to build any kind of support system. Ray said, *"they were starting a safe campaign … just trying things out to see if they would be accepted … but I didn't have the energy or the time and I don't know how to lead groups."*

Lack of time and space was very much a theme. Although student participants often wanted greater connection and community, they did not know how to get it and were often unable to make time because they commuted specifically for a class. Alex summed it up cogently, saying, *"you keep to yourself, you generally don't know anybody … there's not a lot of chance of you ending up in classes with your friends, um and so many older people are coming back to college which is great, but … it is very much, sit down, do your work … that's it."*

Advisors agreed in detail with these perspectives, citing the challenges of working with a commuter group where there was high turnover. One advisor remarked, *"I think the biggest hurdle is this transition, where we just get one year under our belt, and then they all kind of [leave] … there's no continuity between one group and the next."* Another described her efforts to get a group going as uphill, saying, *"[There were] about 20 at the beginning and then it just fell off. After the first year, they just graduate or they transfer to another school or they are only here to pick up a Gen Ed requirement and it's just … or their money runs out and I mean there's a limit."*

Students might feel busy and harried and often not show up, but the presence or absence of publicized support systems makes a difference. Ray said wistfully, *"I do think like an LGBT, or a club would be good umm, because there's people who aren't confident about themselves … not sure, they're not sure … for information or just different information. I see anything in school, I'm just picking it up cause' I want to know what's going on."* The complexity of the lives of students attending community college makes for less participation in the life of the institution. As one ally administrator remarked, *"Community college students [are] wearing so many hats, where you're a student, in terms of your identities, umm that might not be first and foremost, you know, mama all the time, working full time, in school part time, you got all this other stuff that you may be juggling and doing and so, even if the group is there, what's the likelihood?"* Nonetheless, a sense of belonging is necessary in the engagement of students. For those who were not socially integrated into the community college relative to student activities and Gay-Straight Alliance (GSA), they found refuge in the rapport they established with the faculty.

There was a professor and she's also a lesbian and she pretty much helped us with anything. Like, if we needed to come to her just to do schoolwork in her classroom or we needed her to tutor us or something like they were just very helpful. I mean it was more so like she was like a mom to us instead of our advisor ... felt really nurtured by her. (Lisa)

Campus Climate—In and "Out" of Class.   Students spoke about the campus climate as primarily one of silence. One student said, "*I really don't have nothing to say ... except that we were being ignored*" (Lisa). Faculty they encountered were seen as mostly supportive but not considered advocates. Matt, the transgender participant asked in his second year, "*I was getting ready to change my name, um so I approached my teachers and asked if they could switch names [female to male] and they were fine with that.*" Often, this tacit support is insufficient. Lisa continued describing one psychology teacher saying, "*I tried to bring up the whole gay thing and he would just laugh about it ... I mean yeah it's all fun and games, but gay people get serious too. We got problems too.*"

The paucity of perceived support is evident on many levels, and in our research, participants experienced microaggressions. Nadal, Wong, Issa, Meterko, Leon, and Wideman (2011) discuss the ways in which sexual orientation microaggressions have a discernible impact on mental health of LGBTQ youth, lowering self-esteem and producing feelings of shame, sadness, and guilt. Although microaggressions (i.e., daily assaults on minoritized individuals that are unintentional and intentional, nonverbal as well as verbal) occur frequently, most students, faculty, and staff dismiss these occurrences, which invalidates their significance (Balsam, Molina, Beadnell, Simoni, & Walters, 2011). For instance, the LGBTQ organization found they could not get the tent they had reserved at a welcoming orientation because it was being used by hostile organizers for themselves. This incident was explained as a "*personal thing*"—an act interpreted as rooted in a (micro)aggressive act related to their LGBTQ identity. In another occurrence, a poster outside a GSA advisor's office depicting a man and woman in a ballroom dance was defaced with an arrow pointing to the man and the hate word "F----t" written across him, but, although the incident was noted, no institutional action was taken. However, when an instructor goes beyond tolerance, it is often impactful and memorable, which is as much a sign of its rarity. Later, Alex spoke enthusiastically about a philosophy professor:

(He) was a very cool guy, he was very accepting, you know, it was a rule, if you're going to be a bigot, get out (laughs). It was um, he told a story about someone in his class at one point, who had umm come out within the first couple of sessions, like, 'hey, I'm gay and this is relevant to discussion because you know whatever. And he was like, 'and that kind of thing has to be tolerated here because that's what we do, this is a philosophy class, so if you can't be open-minded, you have no business here.

When active discrimination does occur, the route often taken for redress is through personal networks of support. When a student came out
in class revealing her partner's same-sex identity in her presentation, the
instructor declared that the partnership was illegal and went on to humili-
ate the student. The student came to the GSA advisor who in turn went to
the dean of student services she approached previously, trusting that something would be "done on a personal level." One staff member who serves
as a GSA advisor recalled hearing other staff air openly hostile and negative
views on sexual minorities out of students' hearing. *"And when they [the
LGBTQ students] leave, then somebody says, you know ... whatever it might
be ... usually something about flaming, or you know, the biggest F _ g they've
ever seen."* Her way of dealing with it was to self-protect so as not to stand
out and be targeted while still experiencing the hostility as powerful, saying *"To some extent, you make sure when you do things like ... a day of silence
on Friday that you do it as a group. Because if you happen to run into one of
those people and it's ... you don't want to offend them because they may have
ties higher up the totem pole."*

The most glaring indication of this lack of institutionalization of
LGBTQ affirmation in community college settings also seemed the least
actively noticed by participants. Ben shared, *"I would love to see learning
beyond the classroom credits at the community college that can help queer the
curriculum."* In interview after interview, the interviewers would ask about
the academic integration of content to be met with bewilderment and, even-
tually, a disclosure of either ignorance of any such content or dawning
awareness that it was lacking. Other than one faculty member, participants
did not spontaneously address the academic mission and focus of the institution or question the lack of LGBTQ coverage. This GSA advisor declared
flatly, *"We have no women's studies, gender identity, or gender studies, LGBTQ
studies no sexuality, no LGB course. We have none of those."* More often, when
asked about academics, the response would be, *"Well, there is a Sociology
of Sex Roles class that is on the books."* Moreover, another faculty member
offered, *"it's often not offered, I mean I don't think it's been offered, it may not
have been offered on this campus since I've been here which is 18 years."*

The search for explanations for this phenomenon included a sense that
the primary academic mission of community colleges was to get students
prepared for college, that courses in gender and sexuality were junior and
senior level and did not have much of a place in 2-year institutions that
focused more on general education and vocational training or that students
did not want such courses. On the other hand, while student participants
did not ask for such content, when they were prompted and asked if they
would be interested, they were usually enthusiastic. Alex said, *"A women
and gender course would be great!"* An administrator discussed this singular-
ity by saying that curricular change would be extraordinarily difficult given
the powerful faculty. *"In my mind's eye looking at a conference room with all
those department chairs of the campus sitting around and all this gray hair, and*

all these, you know, potbellied old men, and yeah, I know, yes, I am includ-
ing them … so the power structure within the faculty, frozen at the level of the
department chairs is very old, very staid, and not particularly [supportive]."
It was much easier to install cocurricular support services than to have the
academic mission of the institution acknowledge gender and sexuality as
valid and legitimate, even central aspects of student lives.

Given that community colleges have a central academic mission, the
implication of the lack of gender and sexuality courses is that such content
is intellectual and less real world than the general education courses that
are bread and butter and necessary. Learning about the context of people's
lives is important for general history but has little to do with the academic
mission, which is primarily a remedial preparation that is divorced from
intersecting minority identities.

Personal History and Intersecting Identities.   One emerging theme
for many of the students we interviewed was the importance of reconciling
religion and identification as LGBTQ. Several of the students were raised
in devout Christian homes. A few students were "out" on campus but re-
treated to being the son or daughter who reflected the Christian values and
norms that their families expected. Hence, the community college context
provided a respite for some of our participants who were largely traditional
college-age students who were still heavily dependent on their parents. One
young woman explained:

> I grew up in a very restrictive household—very conservative Christian
> parents—and conservative Christian family and there was never any encour-
> agement to explore, outside of heterosexual boundaries. Yeah … that's pretty
> much it. Like, they—my parents basically believe that bisexual or anything
> aside from heterosexual is wrong or something —something must be wrong
> with me to identify that way—to identify as bisexual. And … so I haven't
> come out to my parents yet. I've—I've come out to a couple close friends and
> to my boyfriend and … that's —about as far as it got and I don't think I will
> tell my parents. Mostly because I'm worried they would—until I'm financially
> independent they … could take potentially a whole college experience away
> from me. (Bristol)

In terms of intersectionality, many students cited religion as an important intersecting self. Only one student from the mainstream middle-class,
male, dominant culture indicated an awareness of being gay being different
for members of underrepresented racial/ethnic groups. As Colin discussed
the realities of his membership in multiple microcultural groups, he acknowledged that his minority status as a gay does not erase his male or
white privilege. He asserts:

> To people outside the community I would say I'm gay but really it is com-
> plicated. In truth, my sexuality is more fluid. I don't particularly like the
> labels, but queer identity fits too. Intersectionality is incredibly important

to me. I am a white man; I come from two very privileged classes. But I grew up on hard-core punk, I read and embrace feminist theory, counter-culture feminist blogs … I am aware of active and passive racial discrimination. Intersectionality is probably more important to me because I have this white male privilege.

One 19-year-old student discussed that coming out during her teen years was difficult because of being African American. She expressed that it did not appear as stressful for her White friends who had come out and sensed that there were more repercussions for being gay and Black. In particular, she noted that it seemed the African American community was less accepting and not as tolerant compared to Whites. In recounting the details of when she came out, Lisa shared:

It took a minute, and I didn't come out to my real friends until my junior year in high school. When I came out to everybody that was cause my Mom. Everyone in school already knew cause of how I dressed, but I never came out and said it cause so many people had bad stuff to say. I came out to my mom first. We were watching Ellen. She said she [Ellen] so cool, if I could meet her it doesn't matter that she's gay. I fell for the trip. I said ok, Ellen is my sister, we family; we're on the same team. You get it? She said no. So I went back to my room to let it get into her head. She was going crazy. I braced and she tried to kill me, she started choking me, it took my older sister, took aunts, uncles, neighbors to get her off of me. She said you can't be gay, you are going to hell, you can't be my daughter and just a whole bunch of bad stuff, and she didn't want anything to do with me. So I went to school the next day and she had called my grandmother, everybody she knew and told them. So basically, I went to school and people were telling me that they knew. Basically, I sort of got pushed out the closet.

Approximately half of LGBTQ college students conceal their sexual orientation or gender identity to avoid intimidation and/or rejection (Rankin, 2003). The African American LGBTQ community college students we interviewed discussed being members of multiple marginalized groups. William talked about the coming out process and family/community expectations:

It's sort of harder to be accepted or to be out as a Black gay man than say as for someone who would be White because a lot of African Americans aren't like open minded or more accepting to change or different people and it's mainly because of how they're conditioned and grew up. I guess it kind of goes back to Slavery in a sense. It seems like, in a way, Blacks were taught that other people who were outside of them were the enemy. I'm not sure it's the same for other races too—as far as Blacks. But I think it depends on the individual. If they're gonna stick to that mentality when they grow up and it depends on who did they grow up with and what kind of experiences they went through as well.

Moving from the Margins to Mattering

> You know, you might want to just keep that to yourself ... I mean I'm guilty by association, you know, everybody knows she is a lesbian so yeah, you better be careful ... (Staff advisor)

There were many issues not raised by student participants that were evident in the themes from interviews with staff. One theme that emerged highlighted the compelling personal reasons that staff who became advisors or allies often brought up. This background was not necessarily shared with students but was often the driving force for advisors being active advocates for years with little reward. Personal histories of being closeted and uncomfortable; experiencing homophobia, racism, and gender discrimination; and not being able to speak about their partners shaped these staff experiences of their own identity.

Many faculty and staff identified as being lesbian or bisexual. Some were openly out, whereas others were careful. There was an element of risk in being openly identified, and it is indicative of the campus climate often perceived as safer for heterosexual allies (Goldstein & Davis, 2010). One advisor referenced a faculty leader in Safe Zone training who was "*married and has kids, she's probably late 40s and I said you know, that's interesting that a straight woman is spearheading this. I wish a gay or lesbian person could do this, and she said, you know what, the thing is that with her nobody can question why she's doing it ... they don't think there's any ... ulterior motives.*" The advisor further described how students looking for a Gay Straight Alliance advisor pursued a heterosexual faculty member. She said, "*there are LGBT teachers who they have as mentors and talk to, but they feel, umm, protective of them, where they don't want them to be vulnerable or be accused of having an agenda ... so these kids were actually pretty savvy and strategic around who they selected.*"

Getting Institutional Buy-in and Support. Among the emerging themes in this study were LGBTQ students feeling like afterthoughts within community colleges. Some felt that it was possible to be on the administration's radar or receive the appropriate student support services only through galvanizing to create GSAs. However, some of the students we interviewed did not have a GSA at their school or because of work-life commitments could not participate in the GSA. One of our participants, a transgender student who was a recent community college transfer student, contrasts the climate for LGBTQ issues at a 2- and 4-year institution:

> There wasn't any [focus] ... like here, there needs to be consideration. I mean there [at the community college] it depends ... I mostly used the unisex bathrooms but here it's like first you have the rooming ... you know I don't have a roommate and I have my own bathroom just because that works for my safety and for everyone else's comfort I guess, or something, probably mostly

my safety. Um but um you know so I came out when I told the Office of Disabilities and so they contacted housing so now I haven't really used the Office of Disabilities so now I just contact directly with housing. (Matt)

Conclusions and Implications

This phenomenological qualitative study explored LGBTQ issues in the community college context by exploring the experiences of LGBTQ students and concerned faculty and staff allies. Inductive and deductive qualitative analyses elucidated themes and subthemes surrounding their experiences coming out as well as perceptions of the campus climate of the students and their faculty/staff allies.

Developed over the last couple of decades in gender and sexuality studies, intersectionality seeks to acknowledge and make visible how multiple social identities of race, culture, class, gender, age, sexual orientation, religion, and disability interweave and congregate across power differentials to highlight structures of social inequality and injustice. The construction of these social identities and the ways in which some become more salient and legitimate than others are a process of active negotiation in which individuals both participate but are also acted upon by social, cultural, historical, and political forces. Although it is certainly messier than examining one particular social identity in a vacuum, to then awkwardly join it with other variables, intersectional identities weave a multiplicity of these salient variables in a complex and synergistic manner to be more accurate in depicting the lived realities of LGBTQ persons on today's campuses. For instance, Washington and Wall (2006) found that African American gay men in college are often simultaneously developing a sexual orientation identity, while experiencing a disconnection between their sense of self as queer and Black, with pressures to conform to a restrictive definition of masculinity and conflicts in their relationships with spirituality as well as other men and women. Moving beyond responding and programming for singular models of identity development, educators should consider student identities as mosaics, where dovetailing cultures and contexts are in dynamic negotiation with student needs for affirmation and validation.

One of the major themes that emerged relative to personal identity and histories was the powerful roles of race and religion in reconciling when and if to come out. Familial expectations were significant as many of the students were traditional college age and dependents of their parents, and they were cautious about coming out. Hence, some students were out on and off campus, whereas others felt free to express this aspect of themselves only on campus with the GSA. Race/ethnicity was not as salient for most LGBTQ student participants from the White majority. Therefore, with varying intersectionality, awareness of individual and group privilege across microcultural group memberships differed across the students interviewed.

NEW DIRECTIONS FOR COMMUNITY COLLEGES • DOI: 10.1002/cc

In unpacking multiple forms of privilege (e.g., sexism, heterosexism, etc.), cisgender privilege is a form of transgender marginalization in which the sex assigned at birth corresponds with one's gender identification and expression (Case, 2013). Cisgender privilege was recognized in this study as a few students, and faculty/staff allies, noted a desire for gender-neutral restrooms and locker rooms on campus. Cisgender privilege also emerged as gender identity, gender expression, and sexual orientation were often conflated by those external to the GSA or not members of the LGBTQ community (e.g., heterosexuality identified as norm and only possible option for students, ignoring students' preferred names, etc.).

Students and faculty/staff saw a need for culturally responsive curriculum that integrates LGBTQ contributions across course offerings. Kuvalanka, Goldberg, and Oswald (2013) described some of the difficulties that faculty often face in incorporating LGBTQ material into their existing courses, much less in designing new course content, primarily from colleagues who respond with overt hostility or who invalidating by being passively neutral. By challenging the heteronormativity that exist in classrooms and with cocurricular programming, community colleges can improve education for students across sexual orientation and gender. It is paramount to foster the importance of social justice, tolerance, and equality for all students across the spectrum of difference by designing/delivering curriculum and student support services that are sensitive to the complexity of sexual and gender identity. Students, faculty/staff, and administrators should be called to think critically about how heterosexism and homophobia structure understanding of self in order to challenge assumptions and reinforce inclusion.

The findings of this study illustrate implications for theory relative to performance theory or performativity. Several of the students constructed and performed a heterosexual identity off campus with family. Their performativity or expression did not align with the "self" experienced by others as bared on campus. Having to conceal themselves in certain contexts and disclose their true selves in other settings can produce consequences because they are limiting performance of selves, for the normative heterosexual identity that is assumed to have more value. This performed inauthenticity has real-life consequences that become expressed in a variety of toxic effects on health, well-being, and educational experience. Johnson, Oxendine, Taub, and Robertson (2013) in examining ways to prevent suicide of LGBTQ students, remarked that the LGBT population was more at risk not because of their identity as sexual minorities but because of environmental responses to that identity.

Intersectionality affects performance because our performances of self are shaped and influenced by our intersecting identities. The students who perform heteronormatively do so because they fear the consequences to performing sexual minority selves that are financial and emotional, shaped by a minority racial self that, although marginalized racially, also assures in-group racial support if not transgressed, or by a working class self that needs a familial network of support to cobble and fund educational aspirations. If researchers, theorists, and higher education professionals fall short of understanding that multiplicity of selves driven by social forces of oppression and representation, then they reduce LGBTQ students who come to community colleges as one dimensional and fail miserably to both comprehend their subjective and shifting needs or be able to respond effectively and nimbly.

Community colleges have long embraced the enrichment, personal, and professional development of diverse students. However, not all 2-year colleges have been proactive or progressive in incorporating the concerns and issues facing today's LGBTQ students. The pragmatic approach is insufficient when significant aspects of student identity are segregated into silence and invisibility. Research has shown that LGBTQ students perceiving a poor campus climate indicate unfair treatment by instructors, anti-LGBTQ bias, limited emotional support from family and friends and families' emotional support, and hiding their LGBTQ identity (Tetreault, Fette, Meidlinger, & Hope, 2013). A hostile learning environment for students who bring diversity to campus provides a disservice to the very mission of community college institutions, which seek to remove barriers to learning and higher education. In conducting scholarship on the experiences of students in community college, it is also important to interrogate our bases of selection, focus, and the assumptive world in which we investigate. This NDCC issue focuses on examining and challenging the applicability of traditional college impact and student development theories. However, conventional theoretical perspectives have not been norm-referenced on special student population but instead based on white, middle class male students.

Our study highlights that while there may be some applicability of these theories with special student populations, the theories are not nuanced enough, further minoritizing underrepresented, underserved populations. Moreover, traditional theories of student development conceptually privilege normative students who are generic, not different, and presumably have no special concerns. What ultimately performance theory and intersectionality question is whether such categories of "Special Students" is adequate to accurately represent the LGBTQ student who in shifting selves, stands revealed as Black/female/Muslim/disabled/working class/first generation, with each of those selves adding to a varied representational performance of LGBT identity, or its disavowal. Instead of focusing on defining the "Special Student" monolithically, we have the options of acknowledging that our snapshots are just that, a portraiture that is captured to cohere those shifting selves momentarily in a constellation that will change soon. Our charge is to move our lens to the contexts in which these shifting selves are located, and examine ways in which we can address the needs that drive those diverse performances of selves.

The Gay, Lesbian, Straight, Education Network (GLSEN) 2013 National School Climate Survey found that a safer school environment had a direct relationship to the availability of LGBT school-based resources and support such as Gay-Straight Alliances, antibullying policies, inclusive curriculum, and supportive school staff (GLSEN, 2013). Administrative leaders, staff professionals, and faculty alike can be leaders in creating change in the campus climate (Hawley, 2015; Karkouti, 2015). Their efforts can enhance the educational mission of the institution as well as prepare all students to function effectively in diverse environments such as:

- Initiating and institutionalizing safe spaces for LGBTQ students.
- Developing cocurricular programming that functions on a drop-in basis for busy commuter students who may be as supported by the existence of the programs as by active participation.
- Creating a network of support as well as reward staff and faculty who give of their time and energy to such efforts, are some of the suggestions that emerge from the research.

Finally, if community colleges expanded their curricular offerings to more content that actively engaged with lived students' lives, they might find it evokes active interest and engagement in the process of learning. Students are most disenfranchised when the material they are studying is inherently alienating because it does not speak to their realities. Rather than perceiving course content on sexual minority and intersection of identity concerns as a kind of boutique education, inappropriate to the needs of community college students, a new approach may incorporate and integrate relevant material into courses, and be pleasantly surprised by the resulting enthusiasm of students who see their lives mirrored and relevant. In sum, community colleges are primed to be major players in the recruitment of diverse students, particularly if they expand their definition of diversity programming to incorporate the perspectives and needs of LGBTQ students and offer engaging, accepting, and safe environments for the LGBTQ students.

References

American Association of Community Colleges. (2015). *Fast facts.* Retrieved from http://www.aacc.nche.edu/AboutCC/Pages/fastfactsfactsheet.aspx.

Balsam, K. F., Molina, Y., Beadnell, B., Simoni, J., & Walters, K. (2011). Measuring multiple minority stress: The LGBT People of Color Microaggressions Scale. *Cultural Diversity and Ethnic Minority Psychology, 17*(2), 163.

Case, K. (2013). *Deconstructing privilege: Teaching and learning as allies in the classroom.* New York: Routledge.

Cass, V. C. (1979). Homosexual identity formation: A theoretical model. *Journal of Homosexuality, 4,* 219–235.

Creswell, J. W. (1994). *Research design: Qualitative and quantitative approaches.* Thousand Oaks, CA: Sage.

D'Augelli, A. R. (1994). Identity development and sexual orientation: Toward a model of lesbian, gay, and bisexual development. In E. J. Trickett, R. J. Watts, & D. Birman (Eds.), *Human diversity: Perspectives on people in context* (pp. 312–333). San Francisco, CA: Jossey Bass.

Franklin, K. (1998). *Psychological motivations of hate crimes perpetuators: Implications for educational intervention.* Paper presented at the 106th Annual Convention of the American Psychological Association, San Francisco, California.

Garvey, J. C., Taylor, J. L., & Rankin, S. (2015). An examination of campus climate for LGBTQ community college students. *Community College Journal of Research and Practice, 39*(6), 527–541.

Gay, Lesbian, Straight, Education Network. (2013). *The 2013 national school climate survey: The experiences of lesbian, gay, bisexual, and transgender youth.* Retrieved from https://www.glsen.org/sites/default/files/2013%20National%20School%20Climate%20Survey%20Full%20Report_0.pdf.

Goldstein, S. B., & Davis, D. S. (2010). Heterosexual allies: A descriptive profile. *Equity & Excellence in Education, 43*(4), 478–494.

Hawley, J. C. (Ed.). (2015). *Expanding the circle: Creating an inclusive environment in higher education for LGBTQ students and studies.* Albany, NY: SUNY Press.

Ivory, B. T. (2005). LGBT students in community college: Characteristics, challenges, and recommendations. In R. L. Sanlo (Ed.), *New Directions for Student Services: No. 111. Gender identity and sexual orientation: Research, policy, and personal* (pp. 61–69). San Francisco: Jossey-Bass.

Johnson, R. B., Oxendine, S., Taub, D. J., & Robertson, J. (2013). Suicide prevention for LGBT students. In D. J. Taub & J. Robertson (Eds.), *New Directions for Student Services: No. 141. Preventing college student suicide* (pp. 55–69). San Francisco: Jossey-Bass.doi:10.1002/ss.20040

Karkouti, I. M. (2015). The role of student affairs practitioners in improving campus racial climate: A case study. *College Student Journal, 49*(1), 31–40.

Kuvalanka, K. A., Goldberg, A. E., & Oswald, R. F. (2013). Incorporating LGBTQ issues into family courses: Instructor challenges and strategies relative to perceived teaching climate. *Family Relations, 62,* 699–713. doi:10.1111/fare.12034

Nadal, K. L., Wong, Y., Issa, M. A., Meterko, V., Leon, J., & Wideman, M. (2011). Sexual orientation microaggressions: Processes and coping mechanisms for lesbian, gay, and bisexual individuals. *Journal of LGBT Issues in Counseling, 5,* 21–46. doi:10.1080/15538605.2011.554606

Preston, M. J., & Hoffman, G. D. (2015). Traditionally heterogendered institutions: Discourses surrounding LGBTQ college students. *Journal of LGBT Youth, 12*(1), 64–86.

Rankin, S. R. (2003). *Campus climate for gay, lesbian, bisexual, and transgender people: A national perspective.* New York, NY: The National Gay and Lesbian Task Force Policy Institute.

Renn, K. (2010). LGBT and queer research in higher education: The state and status of the field. *Educational Researcher, 39*(2), 132–141.

Sanlo, R., & Espinoza, L. (2012). Risk and retention: Are LGBTQ students staying in your community college? *Community College Journal of Research and Practice, 36,* 475–481.

Tetreault, P. A., Fette, R., Meidlinger, P. C., & Hope, D. (2013). Perceptions of campus climate by sexual minorities. *Journal of Homosexuality, 60*(7), 947–964.

Washington, J., & Wall, V. A. (2006). African American gay men: Another challenge for the academy. In M. J. Cuyjet & Associates (Eds.), *African American men in college* (pp. 174–188). San Francisco: Jossey-Bass.

EBONI M. ZAMANI-GALLAHER is a professor at the University of Illinois at Urbana-Champaign. She received her Ph.D. in Higher Education with a specialization in Community College Leadership from the University of Illinois at Urbana-Champaign.

DEVIKA DIBYA CHOUDHURI is a professor at The University of Saint Joseph. She received her Ph.D. in Counselor Education & Supervision from Syracuse University.

NEW DIRECTIONS FOR COMMUNITY COLLEGES • DOI: 10.1002/cc

5

This chapter explores the role of student development and culturally relevant theories to support 2-year tribal college student success.

Nurturing Student Success in Tribal Colleges

Loretta M. DeLong, Gerald E. Monette, C. Casey Ozaki

Tribal colleges are institutions of higher education that function within a mix of culture, language, heritage, clan structures, and government unique to the American Indian reservations on which they are primarily located. Since the first tribal college was chartered in 1968, the numbers now have grown to 37 colleges (32 fully accredited), located throughout the United States. A majority of tribal colleges are 2-year institutions; only seven are 4-year colleges (White House Initiative on American Indian and Alaska Native Education, http://sites.ed.gov/whianiane/tribes-tcus/tribal-colleges-and-universities/). Therefore, although much of what we know and read about tribal colleges and universities is inclusive of 4-year institutions, it is primarily describing 2-year tribal colleges.

As the tribal colleges carved a special place in the history of higher education over the past 40 years, the path traveled has been difficult but they have emerged as a study of American Indian tenacity of spirit as reflected in the stories of past tribal college presidents (Pember, 2012). Responsibilities and challenges include inadequate operating funds, academically unprepared students, preservation of cultural traditions within the academic environment, economic poverty on the reservation, and maintaining a positive relationship between tribal colleges and the non-Indian education environment. In addressing those challenges, tribal colleges have overcome open opposition, skepticism, and mistrust to emerge as a major factor in the American Indian survival movement evidenced by the student graduation numbers.

In many respects, the resiliency of the tribal college movement parallels the struggles American Indian people have endured throughout the centuries of attempts at termination and forced assimilation perpetuated by the United States government. Tribal colleges have emerged as a major factor

New Directions for Community Colleges, no. 174, Summer 2016 © 2016 Wiley Periodicals, Inc.
Published online in Wiley Online Library (wileyonlinelibrary.com) • DOI: 10.1002/cc.20203

in cultural and academic success and continue to move forward in the ongoing struggle of the American Indian survival movement.

Tribal College Environment

Tribal colleges were created to provide access and opportunity for American Indian students. Often located in the poorest communities in the nation, they strive to develop programs that provide students with new skills and abilities by employing various strategies that reflect the four facets of the environment that influence student development as described by Strange and Banning (2001).The first of these aspects is the *aggregate/collective* environments. This facet is grounded in the principle that environments are made of and transmitted through humans and their characteristics. The demographic (e.g., race, gender, age, etc.) and psychological (e.g., personality and style) traits influence how the environment is experienced and interactions within it. Second, the constructed environment includes the "collective perceptions or constructions of the context and culture of the setting" (Strange & Banning, 2001, p. 5). This facet reflects the subjective views, opinions, and experiences of individuals in the environment and shapes the reality of that environment. Third, the *organized* environment speaks to the organization and processes that are in place to structure the environment. These include but are not limited to hierarchical structures, policies, and procedures. Finally, the *physical* facet reflects the physical structures and materials (e.g., buildings, furniture, lights, etc.) that comprise an environment.

The designers of tribal colleges purposefully, if not consciously, attended to these facets as they integrated the culture of the American Indian students into the educational design and purpose of the college. This is accomplished by:

- working with elders on new initiatives
- developing new relationships between Indians and non-Indians
- expanding strategic partnerships between Indian and non-Indian organizations
- creating curriculum that meets academic standards and includes rich Indigenous content that reflects curricular content and approaches to learning and student support considered essential to sustaining a successful learning environment for Native American students

Fidelity to maintaining that environment has been consistent and person–environment congruence is a goal for students at tribal colleges.

Within the tribal college environment exists an aggregation of beliefs and personal vital interests that surface among a web of diverse needs, one of which is reflected by this tribal college graduate:

Attending the tribal college helped me to understand how to integrate my education into my life and make it relevant to my traditions and culture. When
I was floundering in my classes, tutors and advisors readily applied counseling. The philosophies of perseverance and patience with the dominant culture and their system was learned greatly from the staff and faculty. I'll always
be grateful to them for helping me attain my BA. (personal communication,
2013)

One example of how Strange and Banning's (2001) environmental
facets are evident in the tribal colleges is the *physical* environment encountered by students attending a tribal college. Regardless of how modest, in
the facilities and campus spaces, students see architecture and design that
reflects their tribal identity. They see signage written in their indigenous
language alongside the English translation. They may see structures depicting totems, tribal traditional homes, ceremonial replications, on-campus
pow-wow grounds, clan representations, and numerous other symbols
reminding them of their rich cultural heritage. Upon entering a tribal
college building students will often see posters and paintings that reflect
the history of their tribal leadership, chiefs, journeys, and in many cases
their own family. In addition, they will see tribal teachings in print with
explanations. They can go to the bookstore where, in addition to textbooks
and college paraphernalia, there is information about their own tribe.

Furthermore, the *aggregate/collective* facet is relevant to the fact that a
majority of the tribal college student population is American Indian. Research has demonstrated that campuses with a racial and ethnic minority
majority result in campus environments that are more supportive, engender
a greater sense of belonging, and promote student success for historically
underrepresented college students. These human characteristics influence
the environmental ethos and experience for tribal college students.

Tribal college campuses and environments are unique in that they
were constructed with the intention to integrate American Indian culture,
generally specific to the local tribal group or reservation, and higher
education (Guillory, 2013). The research and frameworks employed to
better understand their students, environments, and outcomes must
include or be flexible enough to accommodate and reflect their particular
environmental features. Yet, who the students are and their characteristics
are equally relevant to understanding the tribal college context.

Tribal College Students

Tribal college student enrollment was 19,070 as reported in the American
Indian Higher Education Consortium data from 2009–2010. Of those
students 50% were American Indian female, 29% American Indian male,
13% non-Indian female, and 8% non-Indian male. These are the most
recent enrollment data and are inclusive of both 2- and 4-year tribal

colleges. The most recent disaggregated enrollment data are from 2006, a total enrollment of 17,255 tribal college students, with 11,554 of those at 2-year tribal colleges (National Center for Education Statistics [NCES], 2007). American Indian students make up the majority of students enrolled in a tribal college and the average age is 30 years old with the number of females disproportionally greater than the number of males enrolled (American Indian Higher Education Consortium, 2012).

Tribal college students on average are nontraditional according to the demographic definition applied across colleges. The typical student is often described as a single mother in her early 30s. It is estimated that over half of the enrollment is from single parent students. Most enrolled are from the first generation in their family to go to college (American Indian Higher Education Consortium, 2012).

The number of American Indian/Alaska Native students enrolled in mainstream colleges and universities more than doubled in the past 30 years to 19,418, along with the number of associate's, bachelor's, and master's degrees conferred to Natives over the past 25 years. Yet, American Indian/Alaska Natives were less likely than their non-Native peers to earn a bachelor's or graduate degree. American Indian/Alaska Natives account for less than 1% of Americans who have earned a bachelor's degree, compared to 71.8% of Whites, 9.8% of African Americans, 7.9% of Hispanics, and 7.0% of Asian and Pacific Islanders (NCES, 2007).

Although enrollment numbers were not reported by the National Center for Education Statistics for the beginning years of tribal college existence, anecdotal evidence from Dr. Carty Monette, president of Turtle Mountain Community College (TMCC) for 34 years, indicates that student enrollment from 1973 to 2006 increased each year for that tribal college. In addition, the graduation rate of students from certificate, associate's, and bachelor degree programs grew steadily each year, not only at TMCC but at the other tribal colleges across the United States as well (American Indian Higher Education Consortium, 2012). Graduation rates reported by NCES (DeVoe & Darling-Churchill, 2008) for the same year were 90% for students with their cohort group graduating from a tribal college with a certificate, associate, bachelor's or master's degree, higher than the percentage of American Indian/Alaska Native enrolling in and graduating from mainstream institutions.

There are clear reasons for the success of tribal college students. Factors identified by Monette for enrollment and graduation success rate at tribal colleges include local access, low cost, and a culturally relevant learning environment made possible by local tribal control. An array of student special services at tribal colleges is similar to those typically found at mainstream institutions. For example, the U.S. Department of Education funds support projects that provide tutoring strategies, developmental learning, advising, counseling, and services targeting veterans and individuals with disabilities. Furthermore, on each tribal college campus, numerous clubs and organizations support students culturally, socially, and academically. Additionally, there are opportunities for students to travel and compete with other tribal college students at regional and national competitions in athletics, academics and business. Such efforts are helpful, however, too many students are not prepared for college-level work, particularly in science, mathematics, and technology.

All tribal colleges have an open admissions policy and are open to non-Indians. If a person has a high school diploma or is working to earn one, he or she can enroll at a tribal college. A typical college classroom will have an 18-year-old high school graduate sitting next to a tribal member who never finished high school but instead earned a general equivalency diploma. In many instances, parents and their adult children go to the tribal college together. Most students are not academically prepared for college-level work. Additional issues related to culture and language, poverty, geographic isolation, and oppressive government policy contribute to ways that the typical challenges facing tribal colleges are rarely encountered at such high levels by other higher education institutions in serving their students (Shotton, Lowe, & Waterman, 2013). A myriad of theories in higher education focus on change in the internal development of students and the impact of the college environment and characteristics on student growth. Yet, only a small amount of this body of literature addresses tribal colleges and American Indian students.

College Student Change Theories

The effectiveness of the implementation of college student change theories, student development theories and college impact theories, adapted to fit American Indian students served at tribal colleges, can be addressed by learning about the academic, transfer, and employment experiences of tribal college students. There have been studies about American Indian students in postsecondary education; however, most of this research has been conducted on students enrolled in the mainstream universities (Brayboy, 2004; Horse, 2005; Jackson, Smith, & Hill, 2003; Pavel & Inglebret, 2007). Very limited research is available concerning the impact of student change theories implemented at tribal colleges on their students; the few available have primarily been the subject of academic theses (Bergstrom, 2009; Winters, 2012).

Winters (2012) reviewed the work of Brayboy and Castagno (2011), which addressed factors that contributed to the success of Native American students and concluded that student achievement was framed from an individualistic, as opposed to collectivistic, point of view. Of additional interest is the qualitative study by Jackson, Smith, and Hill (2003) of 15 Native American college students who grew up on reservations and were successful in completing college in an off-reservation setting. Emerging themes credited success to "family support, structured social support, faculty/staff warmth, exposure to college and vocations, developing independence and assertiveness, reliance on spiritual resources, dealing with racism, nonlinear path and paradoxical cultural pressure" (p. 548). Similar themes were present in a study of 12 Native American students (Waterman, 2007). Most recently, Shotton, Lowe, and Waterman (2013) edited *Beyond the Asterisk,* the first book to examine Native students in higher education. The authors offer insight into the experience of Native American students, Native American affairs, partnerships, tribal colleges, and indigenous faculty and ways to address native culture and the institutional cultural context. Yet, this seminal publication and the other research described pay little attention to how well foundational theories in higher education apply to and describe this population and tribal colleges.

Some existing theories are flexible and inherent in student services programs and policies in tribal colleges. Schlossberg's (Goodman, Schlossberg, & Anderson, 2006) Integrative Model of the Transition Process is relevant to Native American college students. It reflects the movement of an individual in transition—moving in, through, and out—and the critical importance of the situation, self, support, and strategies, referred to as the four Ss. These Ss contribute and shape how we respond to and address change, internally and externally. As Native students move in, through, and out of the tribal college, the four Ss are important factors that intersect to support or detract from students achieving their educational goals. For example, the strong connection to families and communities, which is an identified success factor for these students, may provide support and coping strategies during a difficult situation. It may mean the difference between exiting college before or after graduation. It could also mean returning to college to continue one's education despite having left college prior to goal completion.

Another of Schlossberg's (1989) theories, marginality and mattering, is also reflected in the application of student development theory at tribal colleges. Schlossberg sought to explain how students experience feelings of marginality when change, such as moving to another location to attend college, occurred. Marginality contributes to the feeling that they do not belong and are unable to develop connections and relationships in the new, strange environment. Students feel they do not matter and consequently may fail and leave. This may help to explain the challenges and attrition that American Indian students have at mainstream institutions. Furthermore, tribal colleges respond to feelings of "marginality" and "not mattering" by implementing student services and academic programs that address student needs and reasons for failure. For example, educators in tribal colleges operate under the philosophy that American Indian tribal culture, history, and language must be integrated into the curriculum to ensure that students can identify and feel they belong and therefore succeed, in contrast to feelings of marginality and not mattering experienced in mainstream institutions. This cultural embeddedness is manifested in the curriculum and instruction where teaching and learning are relevant to the culture of the student being taught. To help ensure that cultural relevance is assessed on a regular basis, a data collection instrument, the American Indian Measures of Success Key Indicator system (AKIS), is used to collect information from the tribal colleges. AKIS incorporates unique measures of success that are not included in traditional higher education reporting requirements. Culturally relevant indicators of success are reviewed on an ongoing basis, enabling tribal colleges to assess the extent to which they are addressing those cultural needs in the curriculum and in student services. By doing this on a regular basis, the tribal college student service staff is able to update services to address the needs of the students and to help them attain success.

Reflection

According to Dr. Carty Monette, who served as the president of a tribal college (personal communication, 2013) for many years, to get to the tribal college requires movement within the reservation, sometimes a long journey but usually a short trip. Along the way, students encounter life-altering experiences that take them to places of growth and success. A student enrolling at a tribal college enters an environment that is welcoming and inclusive. Greeting the student will be a staff person, often a tribal member, ready to offer the necessary guidance. The faculty, staff, and leadership are aware of the student's home and community environment and visibly participate in the celebrations, ceremonies, community events, and pow-wows.

Based on Monette's observation (personal communication, 2013), American Indian students are more comfortable at a tribal college because of visible efforts to address their educational needs. Relevant tribal learning experiences focusing on language, culture, and historical identity, combined with western influence and continuing assessment to ensure fidelity to the mission, separates tribal colleges from other institutions. Students share an atmosphere that promotes an understanding of purpose, identity, loyalty, friendship, and professional responsibility lasting long after leaving the tribal college, an atmosphere that is fostered in the culturally relevant nature of the institution type.

Recommendations

Schlossberg's marginality and mattering and transition theory can be used to position student services in tribal colleges as more relevant and grounded in the cultural context of Native American students. These approaches demonstrate that some elements of college student change theories can be useful and appropriate for better understanding Native students' experiences at tribal colleges. However, there are also lenses that root student services in a local, culturally based practice. At these institutions, in particular, incorporating culture into practice can be a critical element in developing a campus environment that promotes mattering and supports transition for students.

NEW DIRECTIONS FOR COMMUNITY COLLEGES • DOI: 10.1002/cc

Martin and Thunder (2013) promote the creation and adoption of culturally relevant models, such as the Sacred Hoop Model, which is specific to the Lakota, Dakota, and Nakota communities. It reflects the four-phase ceremonial philosophies found in these communities: Calling, Welcoming, Healing (Processing), and Releasing. First, the Calling process aligns with recruiting, admissions, and orientation to campus. Although a tribal college may not focus on recruiting and outreach, how students transition to college in a culturally relevant manner should be a focus. Programmatic features could ensure including extended family, connecting with other Native students, and approaching the transition with respect and integrity. Second, Welcoming focuses on students' early campus experiences. Examples of culturally relevant approaches can range from working to find ways to manage Family Educational Rights and Privacy Act and keep lines of communication open with Native families to providing physical and psychological space for students to engage in culture-based activities. The third phase, Processing, reflects the period of time in which students are evaluating their environment or status and are processing "what comes next." Given the significant percentages of underprepared students at high risk of leaving college, to support students in this "Processing" phase, institutions need to be especially sensitive to students' culture. Tribal colleges are often linked to a reservation; this provides an opportunity for the college to create close working relationships with tribal and reservation leaders. These connections can provide potential ways for students to engage in internships or mentoring opportunities within their community, linking their "processing" about the future to family and community. Finally, "Releasing" students relates to graduation. Honoring their "Releasing" with traditional ceremonies and creating partnerships with campus offices and off-campus employers within the community allows culture to remain a focal point for the student experience. Imagining student services through this lens promotes transition and mattering that are culturally sensitive and grounded.

In light of the connections drawn between adult development and Native American students, transition theory (Goodman et al., 2006) is appropriate for understanding Native American students' movement from a majority to a minority status. A Theory of the Developmental Model of Native American Students from Reservations outlined by Winters (2012) is based upon Schlossberg's transition theory. This theory can be applied to tribal college student services to provide a researched theoretical framework from which to shape practice.

A single student change theory may not be effective in helping higher education faculty, staff, and administration understand a particular population, services needed, or institutional type (i.e., tribal colleges) because the theory was not developed with these populations or environments as the focus. Given this limitation, those working in tribal colleges student services have been blending together and drawing on the most relevant components of different theories to support and enhance the effectiveness of their work.

As institutions that are not extensively included or reflected in mainstream policies, culture, and resources, drawing on multiple frameworks and being resourceful are the rule rather than exception. Student service professionals can use these approaches by becoming knowledgeable about the race, culture, and demographics of the students attending the tribal colleges. This can be supported by analyzing one's framework or lens used to view students in order to recognize incongruities between oneself and those being served. Often simply getting to know the students and listening can inform and guide the student service program.

References

American Indian Higher Education Consortium. (2012, May). *AIHEC AIMS fact book. Sharing our stories—Strengthening our nations through tribal education.* Alexandria, VA: Author.

Bergstrom, A. A. (2009). *JiAAnjichigeyang "to change the way we do things": Retention of American Indian students in teacher education.* Unpublished doctoral dissertation, University of Minnesota, Minneapolis.

Brayboy, B. M. J. (2004). Hiding in the ivy: American Indian students and visibility in elite educational settings. *Harvard Educational Review, 74*(2), 125–152.

Brayboy, B. M. J., & Castagno, A. E. (2011). Indigenous millennial students in higher education. In F. Bonner II, A. F. Marbley, & M. F. Howard-Hamilton (Eds.), *Diverse millennial students in college: Implications for faculty and student affairs* (pp. 137–156). Sterling, VA: Stylus.

DeVoe, J. F., & Darling-Churchill, K. E. (2008). *Status and trends in the education of American Indians and Alaska Natives: 2008 (NCES 2008–084).* Washington, DC: National Center for Education Statistics, Institute of Education Sciences, U.S. Department of Education.

Goodman, J., Schlossberg, N. K., & Anderson, M. L. (2006). *Counseling adults in transition: Linking practice with theory* (3rd ed.). New York: Springer.

Guillory, J. (2013). Tribal college collaborations. In H. J. Shotton, S. C. Lowe, & S. J. Waterman (Eds.), *Beyond the asterisk: Understanding Native students in higher education* (pp. 95–108). Sterling, VA: Stylus.

Horse, P. G. (2005). Native American identity. In M. J. T. Fox, S. C. Lowe, & G. S. McClellan (Eds.), *New Directions for Student Services: No. 109. Serving Native American students* (pp. 61–68). San Francisco: Jossey-Bass.

Jackson, A. P., Smith, S. A., & Hill, C. L. (2003). Academic persistence among Native American college students. *Journal of College Student Development, 44*(4), 548–565.

Martin, S. C., & Thunder, A. L. (2013). Incorporating Native culture into student affairs. In H. J. Shotton, S. C. Lowe, & S. J. Waterman (Eds.), *Beyond the asterisk: Understanding Native students in higher education* (pp. 39–52). Sterling, VA: Stylus.

National Center for Education Statistics. (2007). *Digest of education statistics, 2007.* Washington, DC: U.S. Department of Education. Retrieved from http://sites.ed.gov/whianiane/files/2012/06/Enrollment-in-Tribally-Controlled-Colleges.pdf

Pavel, D. M., & Inglebret, E. (2007). *American Indian and Alaskan Native student's guide to college success.* Westport, CT: Greenwood Press.

Pember, M. A. (2012). Forty years of "fire in the belly." *Tribal College Journal, 24*(2). Retrieved from http://www.tribalcollegejournal.org/archives/25169/print

Schlossberg, N. (1989). Marginality and mattering: Key issues in building community. In D. C. Roberts (Ed.), *New Directions for Student Services: No. 48. Designing campus activities to foster a sense of community* (pp. 5–13). San Francisco: Jossey-Bass.

Shotton, H. J., Lowe, S. C., & Waterman, S. J. (Eds.). (2013). *Beyond the asterisk: Understanding Native students in higher education*. Sterling, VA: Stylus.

Strange, C. C., & Banning, J. H. (2001). *Education by design: Creating campus learning environments that work*. San Francisco: Jossey-Bass.

Waterman, S. J. (2007). A complex path of Haudenosaunee degree completion. *Journal of American Indian Education*, 46(1), 20–40.

Winters, N. C. (2012, Winter). From the reservation: A theory regarding the development of Native American students. *Journal of the Student Personnel Association at Indiana University*, pp. 27–35.

LORETTA M. DELONG *was a superintendent of the Zuni Public School District and a professor of educational leadership at multiple institutions. She received her Ed.D from the University of North Dakota.*

GERALD E. MONETTE *was a former president of Turtle Mountain Community College, a tribal college in North Dakota. He received his Ph.D from the University of North Dakota.*

C. CASEY OZAKI *is an associate professor in Teaching and Learning at the University of North Dakota. She received her Ph.D in Higher Education from Michigan State University.*

NEW DIRECTIONS FOR COMMUNITY COLLEGES • DOI: 10.1002/cc

6

Using India as an example, the authors of this chapter provide background for connecting theory and practice for international community colleges.

Relating Theories to Practice in an International Context

Miriam J. Carter, Francisco J. Marmolejo, Robin L. Spaid

Population growth and labor market expansion have historically led to a demand for education and training. The role of higher education has included the "transmission of knowledge and ideology; selection and formation of a dominant elite; production and application of knowledge and a skilled labor force" (Varghese, 2014, p. 22). U.S. President Truman must have had these ideas in mind in 1946 when he appointed the President's Commission on Higher Education. The resultant *Truman Report* not only presented community colleges as a vital and low-cost segment of the American higher education system (*The President's Commission*, n.d.), but also tacitly promised social, economic, and educational mobility for the masses (Cohen, Brawer, & Kisker, 2014). A visionary policy document, this report laid the foundation for community colleges to serve as the great equalizer, thus reflecting the American ideal of democracy. The principles of *open access* and *equal opportunity* have consequently become synonymous with the American community college.

Open Access, Equal Opportunity, and Theories Guiding Practice

Open admissions continues to be a defining characteristic of community colleges. Since the middle of the 20th century, millions of adults and traditional-aged students in the United States have been provided an opportunity to attend community colleges. Researchers have attributed an enlarged middle class to the millions of trained workers who enroll in American community colleges (Boggs, 2010). This middle class pays taxes, works in midlevel jobs, and does not drain the nation of resources. Likewise, other countries, especially emerging economies, as they strive to

NEW DIRECTIONS FOR COMMUNITY COLLEGES, no. 174, Summer 2016 © 2016 Wiley Periodicals, Inc.
Published online in Wiley Online Library (wileyonlinelibrary.com) • DOI: 10.1002/cc.20204

widen their middle class and increase employment rates, have followed a similar model of diversification in their higher education systems.

Along with open access and equal opportunity comes the American notion of assisting all students with a completion outcome. The standard for higher education outcomes in the United States has historically been a bachelor's or 4-year degree. At the community college level, the public has assumed that this metric is an associate's or 2-year degree. Hence, enter the ideas of *student development, student success* and *college impact theories*, the theories associated with college completion. These three types of theories tend to overlap and therefore, are used somewhat interchangeably in this chapter. In the 1960s and 1970s, these theories flourished. Astin, Chickering, and Tinto conducted research and developed extensive theories to explain, and instruments to measure, student success. The term *student success* has been equated to graduating with a degree.

Today, many retention and graduation practices prevalent in higher education are related to these student development theories. Despite the theoretical bases these models have provided, they were developed for and normed on students attending traditional 4-year institutions. They do not, necessarily, apply to present-day community college students because on average these students are older, often working adults and attend part time. Therefore, the more recent experts on student success write and conduct research about how the college experience affects students and what the impact of that experience has been, as opposed to students and their development while in college. This body of knowledge is referred to as *college impact theories*. However, much of the material for these newer theories is based on the student development research similar to that conducted over 50 years ago with traditional residential students at 4-year schools. This is not a trivial limitation of student development and college impact theories if it is considered that nontraditional higher education students, those over the age of 25, represent 47% of the enrollment in higher education in the United States (Pelletier, 2010). New tools and theories are required to develop programs that address the needs of today's community college students. It is necessary to consider the broader mission of community colleges and the differences between the missions of the 2-year institutions versus 4-year institutions, given that community colleges enroll 46% of undergraduate students in the United States (American Association of Community Colleges, 2015).

Another significant feature of community colleges is related to the degree of flexibility that they have in comparison to traditional universities and the level of connectedness that they must have with pressing economic and social needs. Responsiveness to changing social, economic, and cultural conditions remains evident in the varied missions of the contemporary community college in the United States. "To align with this century, community colleges must adapt, forecast changes, and be creative with their solutions to higher education in an incongruous world" (Roueche, Richardson, Neal, &

Roueche, 2008, p. 1). The flexibility of community colleges and their ability to adapt to market conditions have set them apart from universities (Brint, 2003). At the same time, extant economic interdependencies and technological advances have focused a spotlight on community college workforce development and vocational training programs, especially considering that many of these programs are short-cycle training and over the years, they have contributed to developing the middle class. In fact, currently 60% of American community college programs are vocational or technology oriented. All of these factors have generated increased interest in the role of community colleges not only locally but also abroad. This may explain why growing demand for a competent, competitive workforce also underscores international interest in the American community college model (Boggs, 2010).

Although the concept and name of *community college* can be seen as an American innovation, the existence of short-cycle programs is increasingly popular globally (see Table 6.1).

Table 6.1   Short-Cycle Programs in Selected Countries

Country	Name of Program
Australia	Associate diploma or advanced certificate
Brunei	Higher national diploma
Cambodia	Associate degree
Canada	Associate degree
France	Brevet de techniciens supérieurs
India	Associate degree and competency skill diploma
Mexico	Técnico superior universitario
Norway	Toårige fagskoleutdanning
Saudi Arabia	Intermediate general diploma
United States	Associate degree

This has led to establishing a unique category for the short-cycle programs in the International Standard Classification of Education (ISCED), which is the officially defined reference used globally by UNESCO for organizing educational programs and related qualifications by levels. This system includes the ISCED Level 5 in reference to *short-cycle tertiary education* for practically based and occupationally specific programs preparing students to enter the labor market that also may provide a pathway to other tertiary education programs with duration of up to three years(OECD, 2015). Although the UNESCO classification system is useful for the sake of discussion, when comparing countries and higher education systems there may not be an exact fit because of the specific characteristics of each of the programs. For instance, that is the case of the comparability of the U.S. associate's degree with its counterpart in India. Whereas the American associate's degree carries transfer credits or relates to a specific number of credit hours, India has developed a flexible community college offering both diplomas

NEW DIRECTIONS FOR COMMUNITY COLLEGES • DOI: 10.1002/cc

and associate degrees with the goal of making them more suitable to the emerging needs of a rapidly changing workforce.

The need for a diversified higher education system not only focusing on universities but including the availability of 2-year degrees and short-cycle courses offered on the equivalent to a community college degree is magnified tenfold in countries with sizable populations of young adults and rising unemployment among formally educated populations (Altbach & Knight, 2007). This is particularly true in emerging economies in which the traditional university system is incapable of coping with the rising demand for skilled individuals. At the same time, the challenge of such a diversified higher education system no longer can be confined within national boundaries considering that globalization and expanding knowledge-based economies are among the factors contributing to skills gaps and skills mismatches between today's workplace requirements and job seekers (Agrawal, 2012). Thus, short-cycle education and competency-based training programs aligned with labor market requirements are most practical for meeting current and future global workforce requirements. Community colleges, their equivalent, and alternative similar institutions worldwide are increasingly expected to have a greater share of the postsecondary enrollment. These institutions will contribute to reimagining the workforce development, career, and vocational missions to offer relevant programs with multiple entry and exit points for diverse populations with varied education and training needs and goals. However, such increased institutional diversification in different countries, including the United States, is not exempt from significant difficulties associated with lower funding per student, higher dropout rates, limited pathways for students interested in pursuing further studies, and a prevalent social stigma, among others. Certainly, student success theories not properly adapted to the unique needs of community college students, and the corresponding programs established in institutions, contribute to a limited understanding of the usefulness of theories in adequately supporting students.

The Role of Theory in Emerging Community Colleges

Student development and student success theories along with college impact theories, have historically shaped the work of student services professionals in the United States. More recently, college impact theories have been the focus of much of the research in U.S. higher education because this body of theories focuses more directly on how college affects students and the effect of the programs and services targeted toward keeping students in school to completion. A review of the literature revealed that outside of the United States, there is a paucity of research on student services and theories that relate to students attending ISCED Level 5 academic programs. This chapter revisits the relevance and applicability of student development, student success, and college impact theories in U.S. community colleges with an exploratory reference to students enrolled in equivalent programs in India. The lens used to review the relevance and application of college impact theories locally and abroad is Maslow's Hierarchy of Needs.

Developing a better understanding of the way community colleges or their equivalent operate in different countries is a useful comparative exercise. This pertains to the applicability of these theories. As expected, American community colleges and their personnel have an endemic bias toward the American ideal—democracy for all, upward mobility, and individualism. However, this ideal may be creating an ethnocentric bias about the reasons students attend college and may not be fully applicable to educational systems abroad in which other ideals may prevail. Moreover, although standards of living are varied in many countries in comparison with the United States, it seems appropriate to view ideas about the benefits of postsecondary education through the lens of Maslow's hierarchy (1943) considering that regardless of differential welfare levels in all countries, the ultimate goal of education for individuals seems to be similar.

Maslow defined a set of needs that individuals in general attempt to fulfill on a hierarchical level (see Figure 6.1). Studies have shown that although Maslow's ideas are not fully applicable in the same order or level of importance in all cultures, the lowest levels of his hierarchy seem to have universal application. Tay and Diener (2011) suggested that Maslow's Level 1, physiological needs, appears to apply universally. In addition, they found that Level 2, safety and security needs, is also somewhat applicable throughout the world.

Figure 6.1.   Maslow's Hierarchy of Needs (1943)

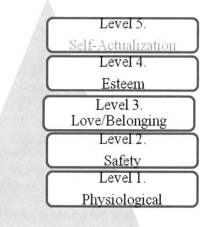

It seems evident that students in emerging countries seeking the equivalent to a community college education may differ from U.S. students because of cultural and economic conditions. Using Maslow's Levels 1 and 2 as a lens to view the motivation of students in India to achieve success at community colleges, the authors of this chapter offer a cogent argument for creating approaches that are different from current completion strategies. We contend that these strategies should be based on concepts other than the tenets created in the United States in which, as indicated before, there may prevail a bias toward a traditional student development approach.

India as a Case Study

India has the second largest higher education student enrollment worldwide, and it is expected to have the largest globally in the next decade once it surpasses China. Currently, more than 28 million students are enrolled in a highly diversified arrangement of more than 35,000 higher education institutions in India, in comparison with 21 million students enrolled in 4,300 U.S. higher education institutions. Nevertheless, the gross enrollment rate in higher education in India is only 24.7% in comparison with 89% in the United States (British Council, 2015). Over the next 10 years, the country will have the largest youth population in the world with the potential to contribute significantly to the global workforce (Narayanan, 2014). Concerns about the lack of job readiness of graduates in India for domestic and international labor markets have sparked calls for higher education reforms. This discussion contributed to the creation of a new type of institution officially named "community colleges," which now are part of the already highly diversified higher education system in India. Community colleges were introduced in India during the 1990s to provide mostly poor, rural students access to high-quality education to prepare them for local employment. Over 2 decades later, the importance of community colleges as engines of social and economic development is more visible. In 2014, the University Grants Commission authorized the establishment of 98 new community colleges offering diplomas, advanced diplomas, and certificate courses, with duration of 6 months to 2 years. The following narrative on Indian students in select rural-based ISCED Level 5 institutions may demonstrate our premise that the theories used to support the practice of student support services aimed at student success are not universally applicable.

Rural India constitutes over 70% of the total population of over 1 billion people. Low education attainment rates and concomitant social ills are disproportionately high compared with urban India (Sharma, 2014). Moreover, approximately 40% of youth start school and drop out before completing 6 years of formal education; only 30% remain through completion of secondary school and less than 10% pursue postsecondary programs (Johri, 2014). Although urban India has advanced, time seems to have stood still in rural India. Blighted by insufficient infrastructure, inadequate health care coupled with malnutrition, poor access to safe drinking water, low-quality housing, and scant sanitation facilities, postsecondary students from rural areas have myriad competing basic needs that affect their academic preparation, enrolment, retention, and completion status.

Conditions of poverty are clearly visible and rampant in rural India. Added to these systemic challenges are the pervasive, insidious effects of caste (King, 2012). Scheduled Castes and Scheduled Tribes (often referred to as Backward Classes) are in the majority. They typically subscribe to traditional livelihoods that have been passed on through the generations. Gayetri (a pseudonym), a community college graduate, is a typical rural student intent on changing her destiny.

A typical workday for Gayetri and many other young women in rural India begins before sunrise. In addition to carrying out routine household and agricultural chores, prevailing sociocultural traditions and gender role expectations mean women are both the primary caregivers for an extended family and increasingly the dominant breadwinners. During lull periods in the agricultural cycle, it is not uncommon to find many women, including those who have completed high school, working as casual or day laborers on construction sites and earning subsistence wages. Moreover, work on most construction sites is a grueling 12-hour day of backbreaking, manual labor often without safety equipment, protective gear, and proper tools. There is often no guarantee of earning the daily minimum wages and no opportunity for training or advancement. These women are labeled unskilled, uncertified workers despite their significant contributions to building India's infrastructure. Their labor is the backbone of civil projects; yet, they remain invisible, dispensable, and vulnerable with no social or economic protections. Furthermore, working in the informal economy, like 93% of all Indians do (Johri, 2014), means they have a negligible voice or representation to improve their circumstances.

The community college model in India is challenging boundaries (Carter, Pollard, & Rai, 2014). Not unlike its U.S. counterpart, this model uses access, affordability, and relevance as key talking points to convince rural students that attending community college might be a viable educational and training option to improve the quality of their lives. Ironically, the provision of student services—as they are conceived traditionally in U.S. higher education institutions—is not common in India despite prevailing social conditions. At a 2012 national conference, learner or "student-first" rhetoric was emphasized as a paradigm shift to improve educational outcomes. Gayetri attended a rural-based community college that operationalized student-centric practices. She subsequently earned a government-recognized certificate in a construction trade, tripling her monthly wages.

Relevant counseling and support services for Gayetri and many rural youths require understanding and responding to the contextual intersection of gender and poverty not from an individual perspective but from a culturally appropriate, communal perspective. Taking the bold and courageous step to enroll in the local community college meant addressing Gayetri's basic needs that included gaining confidence and approval from village leaders and extended family. Providing monthly education stipends equivalent to minimum wages, arranging childcare, as well as offering free and nutritious meals, medical services, transportation to college, internships, and job placement assistance and aftercare were among the strategies to ease the transition to community college education and wage employment. The most influential factors, however, had to do with attitudinal and perceptual needs. Give the vestiges of casts in India, community college interventions had to prove to students like Gayetri that they *mattered*.

Interactions with Indian youths attending community college confirm that that they often feel lost as if they do not exist at all. The open door admission policy of the community colleges starkly contrasts with the prevailing selective postsecondary institution admissions system in the country. However, systemic inequities seem to be accepted: Changing attitudes about who is entitled to postsecondary education and the preference for traditional academic subjects over vocational programs continue to be major challenges. The stigma associated with blue-collar jobs, the implicit *raison d'etre* of community colleges in India, has yet to be resolved.

College recruiters, counselors, teachers, and administrators have to militate against prevailing historic, cultural, and social dictates. Suman (a pseudonym), a college graduate, succinctly stated, "The only consolation in not attending college was seeing so many young people just like me—jobless, hopeless, and helpless." She described the mindset as "kind of like a trauma." Months of idleness and feelings of rejection and being left behind start to settle in. Sanjay (a pseudonym), a current community college student, said he was lost and felt like the educational system betrayed him and his friends. Without social capital (because many are first-generation college students and illiteracy among older adults is prevalent in rural India), several young male community college students described their life before enrolling as "a slow death." Poverty plus hunger cripple the will to even try to return to school, learn marketable skills, or search for work. Because unemployable youth are the majority in many places in rural India, apathy is acceptable. The environment supports it, and failure in and of itself becomes an option.

Conclusion

Many countries that recognize the need for a midlevel technical and job-oriented credential between high school and university are creating programs similar to the U.S. community college vocational or career programs. Currently, at the global level, the higher education landscape is much more diversified, and there is a larger number of countries having a binary system, including both traditional universities and short-cycle technical colleges. These programs are common in countries such as Canada, Mexico, Vietnam, and Malaysia. Australia, Brunei, Cambodia, Saudi Arabia, Norway, and France offer short-cycle programs to meet labor market demands and provide adult students with the skills to fill the gap between labor market needs and skilled labor.

Much of the literature on community college-type institutions internationally refers to the need to develop curriculum, provide horizontal and vertical structure for programs, meet accreditation standards, and the need to develop a vision and mission. However, there is little mention of what students need, as well as scant attention to preparing faculty and staff to understand and support students' aspirations through completion to employment.

As institutions similar to U.S. community colleges proliferate in the world, an opportunity arises to further study the applicability in international settings of newly developed theories around what community college students need. This may help to avoid the risk of attempting to apply outdated student development theories that were developed over 50 years ago for cohorts of students who are not representative of students today. When college student issues are discussed in the U.S. context, generally, the picture portrayed is of middle- class, full-time and late adolescent university students. This has never been the average student at community colleges in the United States. Community college students are older than traditional students, have adult roles in life, may have dependents, work part or full time, and often are in need of remediation. It is likely that the average student in international community colleges will be nontraditional as well. If those students are to be successful both in the United States and abroad, then there is a need to reimagine student services to support these nontraditional students and meet their needs as well as meet the needs of institutions. To aid in rethinking the services, new theories are needed to undergird student services practices at community colleges locally and in different parts of the world.

References

Agrawal, T. (2012). Vocational education and training in India: Challenges, status and labour market outcomes. *Journal of Vocational Education and Training, 64*(4), 453–474.

Altbach, P. G., & Knight, J. (2007). The internationalization of higher education: Motivations and realities. *Journal of Studies in International Education, 11*, 290–305. doi: 10.1177/1028315307303542

American Association of Community Colleges. (2015). *2015 fact sheet.* Retrieved from http://www.aacc.nche.edu/AboutCC/Pages/fastfactsfactsheet.aspx.

Boggs, G. R. (2010). *Democracy's college: The evolution of the community college in America.* Washington, DC: American Association of Community Colleges. Retrieved from http://www.aacc.nche.edu/AboutCC/whsummit/Documents/boggs_whsummitb rief.pdf.

Brint, S. (2003, March). Few remaining dreams: Community colleges since 1985. In K. M. Shaw & J. A. Jacobs (Eds.), Community colleges: New environments, new direction. *Annals of the American Academy of Political and Social Science, 586*, 16–37.

British Council. (2015). *Managing large systems: Challenges and opportunities for large higher education systems.* London: British Council.

Carter, M. J., Pollard, D., & Rai, S. (2014). India and U.S. community colleges. In L. E. Rumbley, R. M. Helms, P. McGill Peterson, & P. G. Altbach (Eds.), *Global opportunities and challenges for higher education leaders: Briefs and themes* (pp. 169–172). Rotterdam: Sense Publishers.

Cohen, A. M., Brawer, F. B., & Kisker, K. B. (2014). *The American community college* (6th ed.). San Francisco: Jossey-Bass.

Johri, S. (2014). Skills development in India: Navigating the labyrinth. In H. Haqqani (Ed.), *India and the global economy* (pp. 120–134). Washington, DC: Hudson Institute.

King, K. (2012). The geopolitics and meaning of India's massive skills development ambitions. *International Journal of Educational Development, 3*(2), 665–673.

Maslow, A.H. (1943). A theory of human motivation. *Psychological Review, 50,* 370–396.

Narayanan, L. (2014). Higher education and the Indian labor market. In L. E. Rumbley, R. M. Helms, P. McGill Peterson, & P. G. Altbach (Eds.), *Global opportunities and challenges for higher education leaders: Briefs and themes* (pp. 143–146). Rotterdam: Sense Publishers.

OECD, European Union, & UNESCO Institute for Statistics. (2015). *ISCED 2011 operational manual: Guidelines for classifying national education programmes and related qualifications.* Paris: OECD Publishing. Retrieved from http://www.uis.unesco.org/Education/Documents/isced-2011-operational-manual.pdf.

Pelletier, S. G. (2010, Fall). Success for adult students. *Public Purpose,* pp. 2–6. Retrieved from http://www.aascu.org/uploadedFiles/AASCU/Content/Root/MediaAndPublications/PublicPurposeMagazines/Issue/10fall_adultstudents.pdf.

Roueche, J. E., Richardson, M. M., Neal, P. W., & Roueche, S. (2008). *The creative community college: Leading change through innovation.* Washington, DC: American Association of Community Colleges.

Sharma, O. P. (2014). Higher education in India: Where are we? *Midas Touch International Journal of Commerce, Management, and Technology, 2*(3), 25–28.

Tay, L., & Diener, E. (2011). Needs and subjective well-being around the world. *Journal of Personality and Social Psychology, 101*(2), 354–365.

The President's Commission Higher Education for Democracy, 1947. (n.d.). Retrieved from http://courses.education.illinois.edu/eol474/sp98/truman.html.

Varghese, N. V. (2014). Overview. In N. V. Varghese (Ed.), *The diversification of higher education.* Paris: International Institute for Educational Planning.

MIRIAM J. CARTER *is the director of OP Jindal Community Colleges, India. She is a doctoral candidate at Morgan State University, USA.*

FRANCISCO J. MARMOLEJO *is the lead of the Global Solutions Group on Tertiary Education at the World Bank Group. He received a Master's degree in Organizational Administration from the Autonomous University of San Luis Potosí in Mexico.*

ROBIN L. SPAID *is professor at Morgan State University. She received her EdD in Junior College Administration from Virginia Polytechnic Institute and State University.*

Student affairs and student services practices are concepts that can replace traditional models of student development, now emphasizing student identity, student voice, and emancipatory advocacy. A new identity is suggested to replace the title for student affairs professionals and student affairs programs in community colleges: student success professionals and student success programs.

Student Affairs: Moving from Theories and Theorists to Practice and Practitioners

Rosemary Gillett-Karam

Lucchesi (2013) asserts that "(s)tudent affairs professionals (are being asked to) forge a connection between critical theory and student affairs as a profession, particularly bringing realization and reflection to how (they) may practice ... behaviors unintentionally" (p. 31). A social reconstructionist perspective asks student affairs professionals to interact with students, not as sponges absorbing the professionals' views, but as partners, ensuring students they can act on their own identities in a just environment. These higher education and community college personnel are the daily managers who respond to student needs and behaviors across many programs and services. They monitor and reform student services, including enrollment management, international student affairs, student government, early alert systems, etc. Their emphases stem from *The Student Personnel Point of View* (SPPV).

The 1937 and 1949 SPPV texts and their subsequent reproductions (American Council on Education, 1937, 1949) describe the roles and responsibilities of student affairs practitioners and student support services. These documents are offered as the *sine qua non* (*without which nothing* or the bases) of student services. We also know the role of student development theory is unalterably related to the student affairs profession.

What seems to be lacking is a critical examination of the fit between student development theories and the variety of students served at community colleges (Patton, McEwen, Rendón, & Howard-Hamilton, 2007). For

NEW DIRECTIONS FOR COMMUNITY COLLEGES, no. 174, Summer 2016 © 2016 Wiley Periodicals, Inc.
Published online in Wiley Online Library (wileyonlinelibrary.com) • DOI: 10.1002/cc.20205

example, Patton et al. (2007) explore how racelessness in student develop-ment theory leads to educational inequities. They state: "Racism can be said to be at the core of a curriculum that focuses exclusively on white, western viewpoints that render students of color invisible in what is learned and discussed in class" (p. 44). They note that student affairs professionals may not learn alternative student development concerns in their graduate pro-grams. These alternative student development concerns are arguably par-ticularly relevant to the community college students and the student affairs professionals that support them.

Community colleges have a higher proportion of students who are mul-ticultural, underrepresented, low income, first generation, underprepared, and nontraditional aged. They are also commuter students, which makes them different from 4-year institution students on whom most student de-velopment theory is based. Many of the contemporary writers who focus on community colleges bring awareness of these issues to the commu-nity college student experience (Rhoads & Valadez, 1996; Shaw, Valadez, & Rhoads, 1996). The examination of student affairs in community col-leges began with the works of O'Banion (1970, 1972a, 1972b, 1972c, 1989a, 1989b, 1997, 2011, 2012).

O'Banion, Student Affairs, and the American Community College

Although some might be tempted to classify O'Banion's works with other student development and college impact models, such as Astin's theory of involvement (1993), Tinto's theory of student development (1993), or Pascarella's general model for assessing change (1985), his works are more likely to prompt reflection and explanation of the practitioner role. Because O'Banion is a student affairs officer, administrator, researcher, and leader in community college research, his works derive from "being there, doing that."

In the text, *Student Personnel Work* (1970), O'Banion chose to concen-trate on community colleges, their students, student services, and student affairs. Unlike the battery of psychological and sociological theories of stu-dent development (e.g., human growth and development theory [Keyser, 1984]), O'Banion focused primarily on student affairs and student services and used such theories to aid student personnel professionals and coun-selors. He employed the works of Raines' (1964), League for Innovation in Community Colleges, the American Association of Community Col-lege, Boyer's 1997 National Commission on the Future of Community Col-leges, and the American Council of Education's *The Student Personnel Point of View* (1937, 1949) to explain the community college idea of student development.

O'Banion's emphases on the community college and its students began in the early 1970s (*Teachers for Tomorrow: Student Development Programs in the Community Junior College* [Deegan & O'Banion, 1989]). In each of these works, student development professionals are introduced as human development facilitators and the community college emphasis is on student centeredness. Unsatisfied with earlier evaluations of student services, O'Banion dedicated much of his own capabilities to righting that criticism and to reflecting on the changing world of community colleges and their students.

Concurring with Senge (1990), the Wingspread group on higher education (1993), and Barr and Tagg (1995) O'Banion explained that colleges needed to put student learning first and at the center of higher education. He declared that community colleges must provide educational experiences for learners *anyway, any place, anytime*. A learning-centered institution was proposed based on six principles: creating substantive change in individual learners, engaging learners as full partners in the learning process, assisting learners to form and participate in collaborative learning activities, interpreting the needs of the learner by learning facilitators, and measuring success by assessment and collection of data.

O'Banion wrote that the learning college does not attack teaching and faculty; rather, it suggests an emancipation of role- and place-bound isolationism and discipline expertise—*faculty do what faculty do best with what students need*. No doubt this is only part of the reason, he, as the only community college scholar, was one of 11 national higher education leaders designated an *idea champion*. His newest ideas about community colleges recognize the completion agenda imperative. In an article titled *Learning, Teaching, and College Completion*, O'Banion (2012) suggested, "Leaving behind the wars of teaching versus learning, community college educators can now capitalize on a new synthesis—the purpose of teaching is improved and expanded learning, the outcome of which is effective teaching—to address a new national agenda, college completion" (p. 15).

Tying O'Banion's works and ideas together in this chapter illustrates changing times and ideas about student development and student affairs. In an effort to trace student development, I envisioned a historical analysis and criticism of theory. Although my attempts to involve community college works focused on critiques of student development theory (Chapter 1) and O'Banion's works from 1970 to the present, I found that mere explanations of who community colleges students are or surveys tied to student affairs in community colleges (Helfgot & Culp, 2005) suffer the same inertia as occurs in 4-year institutions.

A New Focus for Community College Students

In a 2014 *New Directions for Community Colleges*, Ozaki and Hornak focused on excellence in student affairs and the practice of integrating academic and student affairs. This practice is promising from a community college point of view, as research about the practice is just emerging. This focus is on leadership and students affairs. In this chapter, I remain concerned with students and student affairs. For example, limited research on community college students focuses on multiple student identities, the uniqueness of community college students and their special needs, student personnel practitioners, and institutional services; all remain a reason to call for more focused research and recommendations for change. Community colleges as institutions said to reflect their communities can reexamine the needs of their students by *unlearning and relearning* what is relevant for the changing community college student identity.

In a recent speech on diversity I delivered to Stevenson University, I discussed the concepts of unlearning and relearning. By clinging to what we have learned, I explained, we discount what we can learn. Shor (1980) explained that critical pedagogy is composed of "habits of thought, reading, writing, and speaking which go beneath surface meaning ... to understand deep meaning, root causes, social context, ideology, and personal consequences of actions and discourse" (p. 12). Relationships between teaching and learning form a process that involves unlearning, learning, relearning, reflection, and evaluation, especially when considering disenfranchised students. Originally attributed to Freire (1970), critical pedagogy and the reexamination and reconstruction of curriculum as learning undergird the science and art of teaching and learning. Mimicry is decried, and student affairs personnel are expected to connect through shared power, experience, and reflection.

To transform community college student affairs, professionals, and personnel are asked to seek a new path to identify, challenge, and redress issues of marginalization of power, privilege, and subjugation in society and in the classroom. Emancipatory advocacy is expected in a just college environment. There is not one way or one right way to learn. We can deconstruct our own learning to question the relationship between what we have been taught and what we need to know. We can understand that power and privilege subjugate and oppress people who have neither. We can reflect on the idea of voicelessness and what that does to the human psyche and to human agency. We can enable discussions on community college campuses that question the impact of language as privileged conceptualizations of reality and we can question theory as a construct of discourse communities, which has prevented voice and identity of marginalized groups. We can work to marry student development theory and models to student services and diminish the rift between academic and student affairs programs. We can emphasize the need for a new kind of training for student affairs professionals in our colleges and universities. And community colleges that represent the new student and new student identities can lead the way.

Trends and innovation without accompanying critical pedagogy are insufficient for student development or as the base for student services. In community colleges, our questions are concerned with knowing and acting on the needs of the 21st century student who represents a new, emerging, representative, and democratic American. Community colleges can formulate and demonstrate a more modern and inclusive path for student services as the innovators they have been and can be. Suggestions for innovations in the community college and its student support services include and are imperative to:

- Question everything and everyone. Return to curiosity as the basis for learning and to democratic idealism as the basis for social exchange.
- Examine the concepts of unlearning and relearning as a continuous dialectic for learning and teaching.
- Know that student identity is complex and not parsed out as a single characteristic of class or race or gender.
- Practice allowing students to infer, reflect, and posit experiences mixed with their classroom learning.
- Read and reflect the ideas of scholars who now challenge the student development theory discourse preached for decades and based on students who no longer look or behave in the "one right way."
- Look to all constituencies of the college to begin the conversation started in this chapter and bring reform-based community college students' diverse identities.
- Let leadership emanate from the students to the faculty, staff, administration, and boards of trustees.

Like most community college challenges, student development and student services deserve a second look, quintessentially imprinted by the innovations of the American community college. In this article, we have raised two historical rifts in student development theory in higher education—the loss of the faculty role in student affairs and the difficulty of translating student development theory into practice. Perhaps because of its emphases on faculty–student relationships, the community college resolves the first rift. It must also then attune its student affairs practitioners with the tools to overcome the rift of outdated and hegemonic theory that may seek to standardize new community college students who cannot be compared to the traditional identity of students. Rather community college students are first generation, poor, working class, nontraditional aged, minority-majority, veterans, underprepared, and measured by their cultural capital and not democratic ideals and social justice. Because this is our reality, community colleges cannot capitulate to outdated theories based on outdated student characteristics. This becomes a clarion call to student services personnel and to innovation as regularly implemented by community college researchers and leaders.

Recommendations

1. Require in-house training for community college practitioners to reflect and practice new skills as regards new student diverse identities.

2. Expect that graduate programs in student affairs and services refocus their teaching and training emphases to reflect the changes in the new American college student.
3. Appeal to college and university administrators to reexamine and relearn that diversity and student representativeness is a national phenomenon that is affecting the future of all Americans.
4. Ensure that student voice is an integral part of decision making in colleges and universities.
5. Reidentify student affairs staff and programs in community colleges: New names—student success professionals and student success programs.
6. Write a new SPPV document (last written in 1987) that endorses and advocates for these new identities for staff and programs in present-day student affairs.

References

American Council on Education. (1937). *The student personnel point of view* (American Council on Education Studies, series 1, vol. 1, no. 3). Washington, DC: Author. Retrieved from http://www.myacpa.org/files/student-personnel-point-view-1937.pdf.

American Council on Education. (1949). *The student personnel point of view* (rev. ed.). Washington, DC: Author. Retrieved from https://www.naspa.org/images/uploads/main/Student_Personnel_Point_of_View_1949.pdf.

Astin, A. (1993). *What matters in college? Four critical years.* San Francisco: Jossey-Bass.

Barr, R., & Tagg, J. (1995). From teaching to learning: A new paradigm for undergraduate education. *Higher Education*—Paper 60. Retrieved from http://digitalcommons.unomaha.edu/slcehighered/60.

Boyer, E. (1997). *National commission of the future of community colleges.* New York: Harper & Row.

Deegan, W. L., & O'Banion, T. (Eds.). (1989). *New Directions for Community Colleges: No. 67. Perspectives on student development.* San Francisco: Jossey-Bass.

Freire, P. (1970). *Pedagogy of the oppressed.* NY: Continuum.

Helfgot, S. R., & Culp, M. M. (Eds.). (2005). *New Directions for Community Colleges: No. 131. Community college student affairs: what really matters.* San Francisco: Jossey-Bass.

Keyser, J. (1984). *Student development.* Washington, DC: National Council on Student Development.

Lucchesi, M. L. (2013). Hegemony within student affairs: The interpretive nature of college student development theory. College of Education Theses and Dissertations. Paper 47. DePaul University. Retrieved from http://via.library.depaul.edu/soe_etd/47.

O'Banion, T. (1970). *Student personnel work.* League of Innovation.

O'Banion, T. (1972a). An academic advising model. *American Association of Junior Colleges Journal, 42,* 62–64.

O'Banion, T. (1972b). *Student development programs in the community junior college.* Prentice-Hall.

O'Banion, T. (1972c). *Teachers for tomorrow.* Tucson: University of Arizona Press.

O'Banion, T. (1989a). *Perspectives on student development.* New Directions for Community Colleges. SF: Jossey-Bass.

O'Banion, T. (1989b). *Innovation in the community college.* New York: American Council on Education.

O'Banion, T. (1994/2011). *Focus on learning*. Phoenix: League for Innovation in the Community College.

O'Banion, T. (1997). *A learning college for the 21st century*. Phoenix: Oryx.

O'Banion, T. (2012). *Learning, teaching, and college completion*. Phoenix: League for Innovation.

Ozaki, C., & Hornak, A. (2014). Excellence within student affairs: Understanding the practice of integrating academic and student affairs. In C. Ozaki & A. Hornak (Eds.), *New Directions for Community Colleges: No. 166. Supporting student affairs professionals* (pp. 79–84). San Francisco: Jossey-Bass.

Pascarella, E. T. (1985). College environment influences on learning and cognitive development. In J. C. Smart (Ed.), *Higher education: Handbook of theory and research* (Vol. 1, pp. 1–61). New York: Agathon.

Patton, L. D., McEwan, M., Rendón, L., & Howard-Hamilton, M. F. (2007). Critical race perspectives in theory in student affairs. In S. R. Harper & L. D. Patton (Eds.), *New Directions for Student Services: No. 120. Responding to the realities of race on campus* (pp. 39–53). San Francisco: Jossey-Bass.

Raines, H. (1964/1977). *My soul is rested*. New York: Putnam.

Rhoads, R., & Valadez, J. (1996). *Democracy, multiculturalism and the community college: A critical perspective*. New York: Garland.

Senge, P. (1990). *The fifth discipline: The art and practice of the learning organization*. New York: Doubleday.

Shaw, K., Valadez, J., & Rhoads, R. (1999). *Community Colleges as cultural texts*. New York: SUNY.

Shor, I. (1980). *Critical teaching in everyday life*. Boston: South End Press.

Student Personnel Point of View–SPPV (1937, 1949, 1975, 1987). DC: American Council on Education.

Tinto, V. (1993). *Learning college: Rethinking the causes and cares of student attrition*. Chicago: University of Chicago Press. (Original work published 1987).

Wingspread group on higher education. (1993). *An American imperative: Higher expectations for higher education*. Racine, WI: Johnson Foundation.

ROSEMARY GILLETT-KARAM, *Ph.D. is the Program Director of the Community College Leadership Doctoral/Masters Program at Morgan State University. She received her Ph.D. from the University of Texas, Austin.*

The coeditors for this volume synthesize key propositions from the volume chapters and offer recommendations for community colleges to employ college impact theories in student affairs practice.

Anticipating Practices and Theories in the Future

Robin L. Spaid, C. Casey Ozaki

In this volume of *New Directions for Community Colleges*, we offer insights into the roles and applicability of foundational student development and college impact literature for work with the community college student. In the Editors' Notes, the editors posed two questions that served to guide the discussion and inquiry throughout this volume's chapters: If theories and concepts are tools for student services personnel, but have not been developed with and for the student services personnel and populations at community colleges, how well do current models apply to and serve the professionals using these tools? If they are not applicable, what conceptual and theoretical tools do community college professionals have to assist them and the students they serve? Each chapter addressed these questions from a different perspective. Some authors, such as Gillett-Karam and Ozaki, seek to deeply explore the assumptions and basis of the literature in light of community college student characteristics and missions. Others, like DeLong, Monette, and Ozaki and Carter, Marmolejo, and Spaid, examine the literature in relation to diverse types of community colleges. Finally, Wood and Harris and Zamani-Gallaher and Choudhuri focus on specific community college student populations. Both sets of authors examine the experiences of these students using approaches that deviate from "traditional" theoretical and conceptual lenses. In the following discussion, we briefly review the highlights of each chapter and then propose threads and themes that weave across the volume. We conclude with recommendations for practice.

Chapter Summaries

In Chapter 1, Gillett-Karam sets the tone for the volume in her discussion on moving from student development to student success and her reflection

NEW DIRECTIONS FOR COMMUNITY COLLEGES, no. 174, Summer 2016 © 2016 Wiley Periodicals, Inc.
Published online in Wiley Online Library (wileyonlinelibrary.com) • DOI: 10.1002/cc.20206

on theory reflecting practice. She poses questions about the applicability and utility of student development theories used in higher education to undergird student services. Her examination of these questions contributes to a proposed new vision for meeting the needs of community colleges students and student services, while amending issues of inequality, injustice, and indoctrination.

Similarly, in Chapter 2, Ozaki reviews the most fundamental and influential college impact literature. She examines Astin's Input-Environment-Outcomes (I-E-O) Model and Theory of Development, Tinto's Theory of Student Departure, Bean and Metzner's Nontraditional Student Attrition Model, Weidman's Model of Undergraduate Socialization, and Braxton, Hirschy, and McLendon's Theory of Student Persistence in Commuter Colleges and Universities and concludes that despite their enduring impact on and utility for the study and practice of higher education, the nearly ubiquitous shared focus on the on-campus and social elements of the college student experience tended to exclude elements critical to 2-year college students. This analysis leads her to recommend college impact research that is specific to this institutional type.

Harris and Wood offer a framework for examining student success for men of color. The Socio-Ecological Outcomes Model (SEO) is firmly grounded in the literature and one of the major contributions to the recent literature about community college men of color. Using Astin's I-E-O model as a focal point for explaining student success, their SEO model offers a broader application that accounts for the experiences and outcomes for men of color. By considering the specific elements that relate to men of color, in Chapter 3, Harris and Wood afford the reader an opportunity to reconceptualize past ideas about minority males and student success.

Chapter 4 explores the coming-out experiences and campus climate for lesbian, gay, bisexual, transgender, and queer (LGBTQ) students attending community colleges. Findings from this study reveal differences in how students' sexuality has been reinforced or challenged on and off campus as well as in their experiences in the community college environment. Faculty/staff allies and LGBTQ students' perceptions of community college support services and institutional environment are discussed as well as implications for theory and recommendations for practice. Most relevant to the critique of the literatures used to explore LGBTQ experiences, Zamani-Gallaher and Choudhuri propose the use of intersectionality and performativity as alternative theories and lenses that could be useful in understanding LGBTQ students at community colleges.

Located primarily on American Indian reservations, the 37 tribal colleges include a mix of 2-year and 4-year institutions, with most of them being 2-year schools. Culture has played a major role in the development of tribal colleges, with influences from language, heritage, clan structures, and government organizations. Plagued by inadequate funding issues and academically unprepared students, tribal institutions juggle the preservation of cultural traditions within an academic environment and poverty on reservations, at the same time, maintaining a positive relationship between tribal colleges and the non-Indian education environment. A dearth of research and theoretical models exists on student success at tribal colleges that include, integrate, and account for the cultural influence on student experience. In Chapter 5, DeLong, Monette, and Ozaki promote Schlossberg's marginality and mattering transition theory suggesting it may provide helpful ways for considering the support and coping strategies during critical transitions for tribal college students. They extend this argument further by advocating for the use of culturally relevant models, such as the Sacred Hoop Model.

Chapter 6 provided some context to international community colleges and student success. Carter, Marmolejo, and Spaid assess the global landscape of higher education and the impact of theories that undergird practice. Using India as a case study, they question the idea of the comprehensiveness of the theories used to support student services practice in the United States and how those theories might or might not apply to international community college students. The ideal proposed by Truman in 1947 of the community college as democracy's college could be applied throughout the world. However, for these ideals to be applicable, U.S. community colleges must first *clean up their act* and develop programming that relates to the full complement of students represented in their community college population. For community college students throughout the globe to be successful, the stakeholders must reimagine student services.

As a continuation of the discussion started in Chapter 1, in Chapter 7 Gillett-Karam resumes her discussion of the relevance of student development theory for community college student affairs and student services. She relies on O'Banion's descriptions of the community college student and institution as distinct from 4-year institution populations and settings to lay the foundation for the argument that community colleges and their staff need to be learning organizations and facilitators of learning that focus on the goals of success and completion. Furthermore, Gillett-Karam advocates for the *unlearning and relearning* of what is relevant and important to serving the modern community college student in student affairs units. Drawing on a teaching and learning paradigm, she culminates her commentary with a call for student affairs personnel to employ critical pedagogy in the personal and professional examination of providing student services in the community college context.

Commonalities Across Chapters: Moving to Practice

Throughout this volume the authors probe the intersection between student affairs practice in community colleges and the literature, theory, and models that undergird the field and work of student affairs. Across their chapters, three themes emerge: (a) a need to mirror the diversity found in and across 2-year institutions in the literature; (b) a common critique of the student development and college impact theory and models as they relate to community college students and student services; and (c) the advancement of a literature and theory base beyond the historical and foundational literature widely available and taught. Multiple frameworks, theories, and models are proposed for use.

Diverse Students and Institutions.   The community colleges in the United States enroll the most diverse student body among higher education institutions (Mullin, 2012). That diversity is reflected in age, ethnicity and race, role expectations, and even in college readiness. Although community college students are very different from the 4-year institutions, throughout the history of American community colleges, we have used the same theories to guide our student services practice.

Knowledge and understanding of the experiences, development, and success and achievement of specific student populations at community colleges is a narrow, but relatively unexplored area of research, yet the high proportion of minoritized and underprepared students at these institutions calls for more focused research and theory that serves as a foundation for student affairs and services in this institution type. Chapters 3 through 6 attempt to add to this literature.

Wood and Harris's framework and Zamani-Gallaher and Choudhuri's chapter are both the result of ongoing research designed to better understand and support specific community college populations, in this case men of color and LGBTQ students. Expanding the scope, Carter, Marmolejo, and Spaid and DeLong and Monette focused on institutions that serve populations outside of the typical American 2-year college. Although community colleges are an American innovation, their international spread and common structure for tribal colleges prompt researchers and practitioners to consider offering a community college education within a specific cultural context.

These chapters reflect the diversity of our students and summon all stakeholders to contribute to the discussion on this issue. We can no longer use theories with roots in the 1960s that leave out the majority of our students—the students of color, LGBTQ, single parents, teen parents, men and women with full-time jobs supporting their families.

Critiquing the College Change Literature.   In Keyser (1984), Terry O'Banion, Lee Noel, Ernie Leach and Paul Elsner contributed to one of the seminal works on student development for community colleges: *Toward the Future Vitality of Student Development Services.* O'Banion noted that student services in the community college was no better off than it was in 1964. This document has become a "road map" for student development in many community colleges (http://www.ncsd-aacc.com/defining-a-legacy/). At that time, there was a call for creative change. New ideas were proffered for dealing with accountability, partnerships, resource management, and use of technology. The American Association of Junior Colleges (today, the

American Association of Community Colleges) responded by creating the National Council on Student Development (NCSD) as an affiliate council.

The mission of NCSD is to "promote knowledge, expertise and professional development opportunities; support decision-making based on empirical and ethical principles; and, demonstrate a commitment to the personal and professional advancement of student development professionals" (http://www.ncsd-aacc.com/).

NCSD has been in place for over 30 years. Two-year institutions look to this council for guidance as to how one moves from theory to practice. Yet, most community colleges are employing practices that rely on theory developed for traditional residential students residing at 4-year institutions. In assessing the progress made by community colleges in addressing the needs of our students, we do not seem to be much better off than we were 50 years ago.

In this volume of NDCC, we place the onus on the lack of theories that are logical for use with community college students and the lack of theories that have been developed with community college students as the focus. Both Gillett-Karam and Ozaki make compelling arguments at the beginning of the volume that support these proposed conclusions about the status of the college change literature for community college practice. Furthermore, each of the other chapters grounds their research or scholarly argument in the assumption that current literature and theories in this area are inappropriate or do not suffice.

Alternative Frameworks and Theories.   Student development and college impact theories used by 4-year schools emanated from psychological developmental theorists, including Erikson, Piaget, Kohlberg, Freud, and many more. Although these theories may have been utilitarian in creating student development theories 50 years ago, our authors demonstrate that today they are not effective with community college students. Even if it were useful to mimic the 4-year schools, it is a questionable practice because the community college mission is so different from the mission of senior institutions. Now is the time for the community colleges to rethink their student development past and the college impact theory present and conceptualize a new future for developing ideas about student services practice. There is a need for a broad approach that may be applied to all community college students.

Community colleges must have practical approaches to delivering services to all of their students and that practicality must include theory. Collectively, these chapters provide food for thought, as well as propose useful alternative frameworks and theories through which to consider research and practice. Described previously, the majority of chapters (3–7) recommend frameworks and theories alternative to the traditional college change theories. They demonstrate how different and, sometimes, more tailored theories are more applicable to and useful for community college practice. These arguments culminate in Chapter 7 where Gillett-Karam advocates a paradigm shift in the literature and approaches we use to construct and support practice. Specifically, she argues that the modern community college student and institution make traditional student development and college impact theory null. She suggests that framing the student experience from a success and completion framework and adopting an "unlearning and relearning" approach to practice are critical to effective student affairs and services work.

Ultimately, this volume is a critique of the reliance on traditional student development and college impact theories to guide and frame student affairs practice at community colleges. In addition, this volume serves as a call to fill the void of theories and frameworks that are developed through, with, and for community colleges and their student population. The chapters in this volume provide cogent arguments for shifting the lens with which practitioners and researchers approach their community college students. Furthermore, the proposals for alternative frameworks and theories to draw on in an effort to be more attuned to the community college context, provide a starting point from which researchers and practitioners can begin their own reflective and practice-based work.

The authors for the chapters in this volume present a picture of the current use of theory to support student affairs practices. There is a need for producing and publishing specific literature about community colleges and the nexus between theory and student affairs practices. This literature must be available for use in the preparation and training programs for student affairs staff. When discussing student populations, inclusivity must be a priority in programming for students. Consideration must be given to a transparent agenda of inclusion of minority students, students of color, LGBTQ students, and adult students. A heightened awareness of cultural issues for community college students is essential for moving forward with the agenda of transparency. Changes are needed to the ceremonies and traditions at community colleges that currently do not respect the cultures of our students. The question still remains, is there a single theory that has universal application for all community college students?

References

Keyser, J.S. (Ed.). (1984). *Toward the Future Vitality of Student Development Services.* Summary report of a Colloquim held iat Traverse City, MI. Retrieved from http://www.ncsd-aacc.com/defining-a-legacy/.

Mullin, C.J. (2012, February). *Why access matters: The community college student body (Policy Brief 2012–01PBL).* Washington, DC: American Association of Community Colleges.

ROBIN L. SPAID *is a professor at Morgan State University. She received her EdD in Junior College Administration from Virginia Polytechnic Institute and State University.*

C. CASEY OZAKI *is an associate professor in Teaching and Learning at the University of North Dakota. She received her Ph.D in Higher Education from Michigan State University.*

INDEX

Leon, J., 53
Lesbian, gay, bisexual, transgender, and queer (LGBTQ): community college students experiences, 47; campus climate, 53–55; community college faculty/staff, 50; community college student participants, 50; findings, 51–53; margins to mattering, 57–58; methods, 49–51; personal history and intersecting identities, 55–56; students in community colleges, 47–48; study, 48–49
Lowe, S. C., 69, 70
Lucchesi, M. L., 14, 85

Marmolejo, F. J., 75, 84, 93, 95
Martin, S. C., 72
Maslow, A. H., 79
Maslow's Hierarchy of Needs, 79
Mason, H. P., 38–40
Maxwell, W., 37
McEwen, M., 16, 85
McLaren, P., 11
McLendon, M. K., 30
Meidlinger, P. C., 60
Merriam, S., 17
Meterko, V., 53
Metzner, B. S., 27, 29–31
Molina, Y., 53
Monette, C., 71
Monette, G. E., 65, 74
Mullin, C. J., 96
Myers, I. B., 16, 17
Myers, L. C., 29
Myers, P. B., 16, 17

Nadal, K. L., 53
Napoli, A. R., 27
Narayanan, L., 80
NASPA – Student Affairs Administrators in Higher Education, 12
National Center for Education Statistics (NCES), 68
National Commission on the Future of Community Colleges, 86
National Council on Student Development (NCSD), 97
Neal, P. W., 76
Neumann, A., 17
Nevarez, C., 9, 16, 17
Newcomb, T. M., 13
Noel, L., 96
Nora, A., 27

Obama, B., 24
O'Banion, T., 5, 9, 23, 86, 87, 95, 96
Oswald, R. F., 59
Oxendine, S., 59
Ozaki, C., 87
Ozaki, C. C., 7, 23, 33, 65, 74, 93, 99

Palmer, R. T., 43
Pascarella, E. T., 24–26, 29, 86
Pascarella's general model, 86
Patton, L. D., 12, 85, 86
Pavel, D. M., 69
Peca, K., 18
Pelletier, S. G., 76
Pember, M. A., 65
Penrose, R., 9, 17
"People's colleges," 10
Perrakis, A. I., 38, 41
Phinney, J., 16
Piaget, J., 14, 15, 97
Pollard, D., 81
Preston, M. J., 48

Quaye, S., 13

Racism and educational inequities, 86
Raines, H., 86
Rai, S., 81
Rankin, S., 48
Rankin, S. R., 56
Reisser, L., 14
Rendon, L., 27
Rendón, L., 85
Rendón, L. I., 40, 41
Renn, K., 14, 16, 48
Renn, K. A., 12
Rhoads, R., 9, 10, 14–16, 86
Richardson, M. M., 76
Robertson, J., 59
Rogers, C. R., 13
Roueche, J., 17
Roueche, J. E., 76
Roueche, S., 77
Royer, D. W., 25, 31

Sacred Hoop Model, 72
Sanford, N., 13
Sanlo, R., 48
Schlossberg, N., 70
Schlossberg, N. K., 14, 70
Senge, P., 87
Sharma, O. P., 80
Shaw, K., 9, 10, 14–16, 86